BUILDING BRIDGES

*To my wife Pamela and daughters
Claire and Kathryn and grandchildren
Thomas, Alexander, Oliver, Amelia
and Harry who have tolerated my many
absences and to all the wonderful people
I have had the privilege of working with
over the last five decades.*

# Building Bridges

*Fifty years in business*

SIR DICK OLVER

NINE ELMS BOOKS

Published in 2025 by
Nine Elms Books Ltd
Unit 1G, Clapham North Arts Centre
26–32 Voltaire Road,
London SW4 6DH
E info@nineelmsbooks.co.uk
W *www.nineelmsbooks.co.uk*

ISBN print 978-1-910533-78-9
ISBN e-book 978-1-910533-79-6

Copyright © 2025 Sir Richard Olver

Protected by copyright under the terms of the International Copyright Union. The rights of Richard Olver to be identified as the author of this work have been asserted by him in accordance with the Copyright, Designs and Patents Act, 1988. All rights reserved.

This book is sold under the condition that no part of it may be reproduced, copied, stored in a retrieval system or transmitted in any form or by any means, electronic, mechanical, photocopying, recording or otherwise without prior permission of the author.

The cartoons and photographs have been produced by kind permission of the following: *The Times / News Licensing*; cover, frontispiece, pictures 24, 25 and 27. bp archive: photos 9 and 10. Every effort has been made to identify and contact all copyright holders. However the publisher will be happy to amend in subsequent editions any errors or omissions brought to their notice.

Jacket illustration by Peter Brookes
Jacket and text design, typesetting and layout by Lyn Davies Design
Printed and bound in the UK by CPI Group

# CONTENTS

| | | |
|---|---|---|
| Foreword | | *vii* |
| Author's Preface | | *ix* |
| 1. | Eureka | *1* |
| 2. | Beginnings | *3* |
| 3. | British Petroleum | *10* |
| 4. | Time in the Sun | *14* |
| 5. | Time in a Colder Climate | *18* |
| 6. | Further Education | *24* |
| 7. | Family Worries | *28* |
| 8. | Britoil | *30* |
| 9. | Back in the USA | *38* |
| 10. | Above Ground Challenges | *44* |
| 11. | Running the World | *48* |
| 12. | Top Table | *51* |
| 13. | Making Magic | *58* |
| 14. | *BP Explorer* | *67* |
| 15. | Reputation | *70* |
| 16. | Peak Production | *73* |

| 17. | BAE | 80 |
| --- | --- | --- |
| 18. | Taking the Helm | 86 |
| 19. | Bolt from the Blue | 90 |
| 20. | Under Fire | 94 |
| 21. | Change Agent | 100 |
| 22. | Atlantic Rally | 102 |
| 23. | TNK-BP | 105 |
| 24. | Back to BAE Systems: Salvaging Reputation | 113 |
| 25. | Change at the Top | 121 |
| 26. | Threats and Opportunities Abroad | 126 |
| 27. | Board Changes | 129 |
| 28. | Settlements | 131 |
| 29. | Working for Britain | 135 |
| 30. | The Biggest Defence Company? | 142 |
| 31. | Stepping Down | 147 |
| 32. | Retirement? What Retirement? | 151 |
| 33. | From Global to Local | 156 |
| 34. | Turning Point | 161 |

| Endnotes | 168 |
| --- | --- |
| Acknowledgements | 170 |
| Index | 171 |

# FOREWORD

When Dick Olver asked me to write the foreword to what he said was a short biography, I was both flattered and surprised that he should approach me as our past dealings had been somewhat limited, when he was Chairman of BAE Systems and I was its Monitor, and I knew virtually nothing of his previous life and career.

When I queried this with Dick he rather dismissed my concern and said he would send me the manuscript so that I could read for myself what he had been up to in the past. And what a cracking read this has been.

I had known, of course, that Dick had spent his business life before BAE at BP, but I had no idea of the significant roles that he played in that company over 31 years, working in a great number of offices around the world and rising to become Deputy Chief Executive in January 2003.

This book not only provides a great insight into the man but also the company for whom he worked for so long. Through his time at BP, working in so many positions, all over the world, Dick was a spectator or participant in BP's major times of success and crisis. From his days as an engineer, to his career through the 1973 oil crisis, Dick's account of his life demonstrates an ambition and determination to succeed and achieve.

Dick learned "leadership" at BP and how relationships with people, his staff throughout the company, were so important. He writes "that to achieve success, it was not about hard things. It was actually about soft things. And this had the greatest impact on the bottom line".

When Dick left BP and became Chairman of BAE his experience of senior leadership turned out to be invaluable, as BAE faced criminal investigation both in the US and UK. In June 2007 Dick appointed Lord Woolf to conduct an independent review of the ethical performance of the company, from bottom to top in the company, and the Woolf Report has been an invaluable guide to all businesses and was influential in the Government deciding to legislate in what became the Bribery Act 2010.

During my time as Monitor Dick was totally committed to the 'clean-up' necessary at BAE. Without his support, and that of the CEO and Board, the fresh approach to compliance that I was strongly advocating could not have been achieved.

Dick's big disappointment as Chairman of BAE was the failure to achieve a merger with EADS, later to rebrand itself as Airbus. Despite his incredible skills at lobbying and influencing the key players, even Dick couldn't move Angela Merkel to support the proposal and that was the end of it.

In this book Dick writes with passion not only about his business career but also about his love of family and sailing, where he exhibits the same competitive outlook that I suspect spurred him on to the success he has had as a businessman.

DAVID GOLD
*Rt Hon The Lord Gold of Westcliff-on-Sea*

## AUTHOR'S PREFACE

I WAS ENCOURAGED and persuaded to write this book by friends and family who convinced me I had a story to tell.

The contents represent my personal recollections and comments, and do not necessarily represent the views of other individuals, corporations or governmental bodies.

All proceeds from the sale of this book will be donated to Help for Heroes (charity registered in England and Wales (1120920) and Scotland (SC044984)).

CHAPTER 1

# *Eureka*

It was an advert in the *New Civil Engineer* magazine that changed my life. A recruitment notice for British Petroleum, as it was then known. It looked interesting so I applied. I was called for interview. BP at that time had been recruiting people mainly from Oxbridge. They must have felt there might just be a few bright people from other places. I am pretty sure I got offered a job because I had a first-class honours degree. Throughout the following 31 years I spent at BP I never felt that not going to Oxford or Cambridge was ever an issue. Indeed my subsequent career showed that it was no disadvantage or obstacle.

BP offered me £3000 pounds a year. I turned the job down.

I was already earning £3000 a year at the government's road construction unit as a civil engineer building roads and bridges. However I calculated that I would have to pay more to travel to work at BP. I had a family to feed. I was going to end up less well off.

That just shows how small-minded one can be at 26.

I had known Pam at school. I met her again at a rugby match: I played centre three-quarter for the old boys. That is when we got together. I was at university. She was working. She had been to college to do high class cooking. She then joined a bank to earn some money. We got married incredibly young – I was 21 – and she worked while I was at university. She kept us going while I was studying. We lived in a flat above one of her father's dry-cleaning shops: you never forget the smell of perc. My university course was extremely hard work. We took it incredibly seriously. The programme of six months study and then six months work meant that it was full on. There was little time to enjoy the other attractions and distractions of university life.

*1*

## 1. EUREKA

I was already working when Pam told me she was expecting. Then came the moment when Pam said, I think it is time to go. We went to the hospital where we waited. And waited. It seemed to take a huge length of time but eventually this beautiful little girl emerged. Claire was born in November 1972.

Fortunately, six months after my initial interview BP's head of personnel called me back. By then I had designed the same viaduct yet again. I realised it was not actually very interesting. "You don't really understand", he said. "We are BP". So for whatever reason I collapsed into BP. I little expected that my qualification as a civil engineer would be of much use for long in an oil and gas company. I was wrong.

CHAPTER 2

# *Beginnings*

I NEVER HAD THE education my father had. I say that without any sense of rancour or resentment. It is merely a fact of life. It might also explain why I came to believe so strongly in the importance of education and training to change people's lives.

My father came from a large family with long roots in Cornwall. One of the Olvers, Jacob, was the mayor of Falmouth. His twin brother was head of the fire service. The whole family was very much involved there. They were the Trinity House representatives. They put the first navigation mark on Black Rock. They built the lighthouse at St Anthony in Roseland on the other side of the harbour; the railway to Truro and every station on the route; and the town hall. They owned many houses in the town. They came to Falmouth from St Stephen where part of the family was farming; others were working the white china clay in the St Austell area. It was a big family at that time. When Jacob died, 30 workers from the company and hundreds of people walked behind the hearse through town. Marrying into the Lake family must have been a good move. Because they opened the newspaper, *Lake's Falmouth and Penryn Packet*. It was launched in 1858. It is now the *Falmouth and Penryn Packet*: the Lake was dropped many years ago. Ivan Lake was the last Lake and he died at that lovely hotel on the Helford river, Budock Vean. It was obviously a rather more important family in those days than it is today.

The Olvers were into everything. They were stonemasons, builders, undertakers and purveyors of building equipment. They had property. At one stage my father said they owned all of Greenbank Terrace where the Greenbank Hotel is today. Before the war they were a family of substance.

My father was born in Brentford in Middlesex on 28 March 1917. His father died on 30 September 1921, when my father was four and a half. According to his death certificate, he died of diabetes. He went into a coma and never recovered. He was 41. It was only the following year that insulin was produced for the first time as a treatment for diabetes. My father's newly widowed mother determined that her son should be educated outside Cornwall. My father went to board at Dulwich at the age of six: he left school when he was 18. He had a very good education.

My father's further education was thwarted by the outbreak of war. He had been offered a place to do engineering at King's. Since he had been a cadet in the officer training corps at school, he was commissioned straightaway. That at least is what the family always believed.

However the dates do not quite fit that family story. If he was born in 1917 he would have been 22 when war broke out. He would have had plenty of time to have gone to university after school. What we do know is that he had joined the territorials on 3 May 1939, in anticipation of the outbreak of war.

My father, like so many of that generation, never talked about what he did in the war. We know that he served in the Western Desert, between Alexandria and Tobruk, going backwards and forwards fighting Rommel. The records held at the Imperial War Museum show that Captain Graham Lake Olver of the Royal Ordnance Corps went missing at El Alamein and was mentioned in despatches, signified by an oakleaf on his campaign medal. He then came up through Sicily and Europe after the opening of the Second Front. He finished the war as a Major.

After the war he did consider staying on in the army. But whatever happened, he joined HSBC. Or perhaps he re-joined them. It may be that he had worked for the bank before the war. We still do not know why he did not go to King's: and there is no one still alive we can ask about that. The bank was keen to send him to Hong Kong. For his career he should definitely have gone. In those days employees went on their own: they did not take their families with them for the first year. He had married during the war and my elder brother Michael was born in 1944. My mother told my father he had been away for most of the seven years of the war. This was not the time to go away again. So he stayed. He was an impeccably behaved officer and a gentleman. He did *The Daily Telegraph* crossword every day. The war had taken its toll. He was to die in 1976 of a cerebral

## 2. BEGINNINGS

haemorrhage at the age of 58. The smoking and drinking he took up in North Africa can have done him no good.

My mother was very talented and extremely beautiful, although her hair turned completely white waiting for the war to end happily. Before the war she was hoping to become a concert pianist or a soprano. She played the piano and could sing. She even cut a record of her singing, which my younger brother Tim, born nine years after me, has a copy of. She sang and played the piano and organ all her life. None of this musical talent seems to have flowed down to me or my brothers. During the war she lived in Woodford Green, then in Essex. She must have learnt secretarial skills: touch typing and shorthand although I have no memory of her working.

My earliest memories really were of living in a 400-year-old cottage in the village of Fyfield in Essex. I would go fishing in the Roding river – I am a terrible fisherman – riding my bike or playing in fields and garden. My father had old cars. I saw him once taking the engine out of an Austin 7 and then walking indoors and putting it on the kitchen table. That was not very popular with my mother. We did not have very much. There was still rationing after the war. I can still picture those blue tickets for concentrated orange juice and milk. Tim was born at home and that created a rapid new learning process. My older brother and I did lots with Tim and I remain close to him today.

I went to the local primary school. I was really badly educated and failed the 11 plus. When I was about 11 we moved to Wanstead. My father could not afford to send me to Dulwich. So I went to Nightingale Secondary School. It was a brand-new school and exciting. My father knew the head who was an interesting character. I certainly flourished there. I learned how to deal with anybody and everybody. I ended up as deputy head boy. I played and enjoyed rugby and basketball. In time I did well enough at school to transfer to West Hatch Technical High School, in Chigwell. Nightingale must have been a good school because half a dozen of us went on to grammar school.

I spent time every summer with aunts in Cornwall. We used to drive down through the night. We would go down the old A303 and A30. One of the first things I learned was how to mend a puncture. It was very important because the old cars did not have much tread on the tyres. I do not think we ever got there without making at least three stops to mend a puncture.

My father knew Cornwall like the back of his hand. Our old car used to stop halfway up a hill, while it burned the oil off the clutch plates, filled the car with blue smoke and then proceeded up the hill. I did not think anything about it.

We would go down with a tent on the roof of a car. We would camp. There was no question of us being able to afford to stay in a hotel or a boarding house. We would build our own toilet in the field, wigwam style. It was sometimes extremely wet. I learned a lot about cold water, pitching tents, treading on duck boards, and how to keep dry. Fairly basic things but my grandchildren would not know any of this now.

These were harsh times. When my father came back from the war we had essentially nothing. Whatever family fortune once existed had been dissipated. Olvers once had money, but my father's schooling was probably the last of it. By the 1950s, my father had one house left above Greenbank Terrace. When a retaining wall fell down, he could not afford to have it rebuilt, so he gave the house to the tenant. There were a lot of maiden aunts who lived in hotels. In that era, unmarried women were not legally allowed to own property. They had to stay at home or rent. Either way, they were a financial drain on their family. That swallowed all the money from the Olver family businesses. Certainly I have never seen any of it.

There was really only one aunt who I knew really well. Aunt Maud was a remarkable woman. I would have been going to Cornwall between the ages of eight and 11. I imagined she was 100 although she was probably in her eighties. She used to wear a black costume and go into the sea to swim. I have a vivid picture in my head of her in the water. She obviously swam regularly. That is probably why she lived into her 90s. I cannot actually remember my dad in the water. I discovered that the water in Cornwall is extremely cold. It must have been where I learned to swim breaststroke. I still do not swim very well.

That is also where I got my love of boats. My father was always into boats. I do not think he was ever a great sailor, but he liked sailing. We used to rent a motorboat. Then later on when we were into sailing, we used to actually tow a GP 14 on the back of the car down to Cornwall and sail that.

I learned to sail in Cadets, famous little boats, an international class, on a pond in Essex owned by the local GP. He had a big family, enlarged after the Soviet suppression of the 1956 Hungarian uprising when they took in a young refugee from Budapest. We were family friends. Then

## 2. BEGINNINGS

my elder brother and I bought some crappy boat that we found in a clump of stinging nettles in Burnham-on-Crouch. We rebuilt it, not terribly well, and it fell apart in use. Then I graduated to a Hornet, a racing dinghy with a sliding seat. I used to race a lot at the Royal Corinthian Yacht Club at Burnham-on-Crouch. It was all about dinghies and racing. I do not think Pam liked the sliding seat much!

I started my understanding of cars, I suppose, at a very early age. I got my first car when I was 16. I purchased an Austin 10 for the princely sum of £5 and set about rebuilding the engine and trying to get the cable brakes to work. I ground all those side valves: my mother's father was in the motor trade and he had the most wonderful array of tools. So I was mechanically minded at a young age. I loved tinkering. I took my driving test at 17 in my father's car. By then he had a slightly better car, an old Packard. It was a huge thing, with six cylinders and three forward gears. The examiner asked me to do a three-point turn. I asked him if he would like me to do it backwards or forwards. Somebody told me how arrogant I must have been at that age to actually have asked that question. I passed first time, something that I point out to my grandchildren because nobody passes first time now.

At grammar school, I loved maths and did pure and applied maths and physics at A level. I would have liked to have done medicine but had done the wrong A levels. I would have needed chemistry and biology. Engineering was the next best thing. I did well at school – and then had to think about university. Both my parents had suffered during the war. But they came from upper middle class families and knew enough people who could help. My mother knew a director of the civil engineering firm W & C French (later purchased by Kier). They offered to sponsor me to do civil engineering, as long as I went to The City University, one of the early universities that came out of the colleges of advanced technology. The City University had been created by Royal Charter in 1966. It had earlier been the Northampton College of Advanced Technology, not because it had anything to do with Northampton but because the land it was built on in the City of London had been bequeathed by the Marquess of Northampton. City continued the tradition of focussing on engineering, science, business, management studies and computing.

So in 1967 I went to The City University and was paid £5 per week in little brown envelopes from the firm. Especially coming from a post-war family that was financially constrained this made me a relatively wealthy student. I was on a sandwich course. I did six months study and six months work every year of my four-year degree course. It was a fantastic way of doing things. I was not the only one to think so. Many years later I was at some highbrow event at the Royal Academy of Engineering. There were people of my sort of age around the table. All had made something of their degrees and succeeded in their careers. And 80% of them had done sandwich courses. It was extraordinary. I was amazed. Now students on a four-year course often have a third year out to gain experience in industry. We call that the thick sandwich.

I did the thin sandwich with W & C French. I was a junior engineer on site with a theodolite and a level on the construction of the Tower Hill underground station. I worked in the day and I worked at night. So I gained some idea what working at night was like. I saw everything including whose cars in the morning were much lower on their springs than when they arrived. They had sawn through the underground cables and stuck the lengths in their cars to go and sell the copper as scrap. But it was quite an interesting job. We had to underpin the War Memorial, which involved piling and hydraulic jacks and all sorts of quite technical stuff. So that was a piece of learning.

I next worked on the M18 motorway. This was before Spaghetti Junction was built. One of the last things I did was to set out the Spaghetti Junction foundations. Again, I was a junior engineer with theodolite and level. I also had to deal with materials, the quality of materials and how to build roads. As soon as I could I became a member of the Institute of Highway Engineers, which had been established in 1972, and the Institution of Municipal Engineers. I was the only person to get a first-class degree in my civil engineering group. In those days, first-class degrees were quite rare.

I was ambitious and wanted to qualify as a Chartered Civil Engineer. This required design as well as site experience. W & C French were not quick to realise this. The father of one of my friends at university was the chief engineer for Essex County Council. He was an interesting man. He slept with a machete under his pillow. During the war he had been a prisoner of the Japanese forced to work on the Burma railway. It traumatised him. He would never have anything Japanese anywhere near the house. No Japanese lawnmowers. Nothing.

Essex County Council offered me a job as a civil engineer in the highways department. This was shortly after a number of box girder bridges had

## 2. BEGINNINGS

failed. The most celebrated case of a collapsing bridge was the Tacoma Narrows in 1940. In Britain, the most devastating was when a section of the Cleddau bridge over Milford Haven on 3 June 1970 collapsed while it was under construction, killing five. As a consequence the government made it a requirement to check every box girder bridge in the United Kingdom.

I was seconded from Essex County Council to the road construction unit. Road construction units designed motorways and viaducts and bridges for major trunk roads in the 70s. Bridges were collapsing because the thin plates they were made of were buckling. They just had not been designed with the right codes. An updated code of construction had been sent to civil engineers on how to design box girder bridges. I had to use the code to check all these box girder bridges. This necessitated specific expertise and was quite complicated. It required an understanding of modern technology, computers, and particularly finite element analysis. I had to basically look at the box girder and divide it up into lots of finite elements. I then ran computer programmes to see when they would buckle. It required a lot of computing, which of course was in its very early days. I had already started to use computers. At university there was a massive room with valves in it with less computing power than a smart phone today. We would use cards and tapes. At the time, it was probably the most complex civil engineering challenge. The principles we applied were derived more from aeronautical engineering than from civil engineering.

When I had finished checking all the bridges they asked me to stay on and design new bridges. This was invaluable for my professional qualification. All this gave me the design experience I needed. It enabled me to take my Part III exams and become a Chartered Civil Engineer at the youngest age possible of 26.

The road building programme was winding down. The road construction units were disbanded since they were no longer needed. I stayed until I realised I was only designing the same viaduct over and over again. Then the ad for British Petroleum caught my eye.

CHAPTER 3

# British Petroleum

I JOINED BP IN DECEMBER 1973. It was of course a momentous time. The Arab oil producers had imposed an embargo on the United States and other importing countries during the October 1973 Middle East war. BP's main source of oil was from the Middle East. In quick succession countries where BP got its oil from - Iran, Iraq, Kuwait, and Abu Dhabi - announced either the full or partial nationalisation of their oil industries. Libya even before 1973 had announced it was to take a higher cut on oil that was exported from the country. The industry was in crisis. No company was more exposed than BP. Oil from the Middle East and North Africa plunged from making up 80% of the company's supply to around 10%. However even before being cut off from its Middle East supplies, BP had discovered major oil and gas fields in Prudhoe Bay in Alaska and in the North Sea off the coast of Scotland. But my first job had little to do with geopolitics.

I joined the engineering department in Britannic House North in Moorgate - which does not exist anymore. It was really interesting and varied work. I designed cavern storage in the rocks to store crude oil for the Mongstad refinery in Norway; runways in Das Island in Abu Dhabi; and foundations and the odd bridge. I had gone from being a specialist in box girder bridges to a jack of all trades. Nobody seemed to know how to design a bridge. That was quite useful because I did.

As a civil engineer, one of the first things I did was to go and deal with an issue with the southern North Sea gas pipeline. This came up through the beach at Easington at the mouth of the Humber estuary. I had to tell them how to protect the pipeline. It was a piece of simple engineering.

I once had to find out about getting something heavy ashore in Iran. I

## 3. BRITISH PETROLEUM

had to go to the Geological Society. I met an elderly man sitting there. He turned out to be Professor Sir Peter Kent, president of the society since he had retired from BP. He had joined BP before the war and worked in Iran. I wanted to know what the beach was like where we wanted to land this piece of equipment. He was able to tell me the size of every pebble on the beach. It was extraordinary. I was a young civil engineer who knew nothing about global politics. I discovered quite how deep BP's expertise was across the world. That was when we had the Iran Oil Services Company.

I had only been there a short time when I was asked to go to Calgary. BP Canada wanted to assess prospects for a tar sand mine. The Athabasca oil sands of Alberta contain bitumen and heavy oil on a scale comparable to the entire proven reserves of oil in the Middle East and the rest of the world. The challenge was the cost of production. BP Canada felt they needed a civil engineer to estimate the physical challenges of any mine. I went for a brief pre-feasibility study. When I got home after six weeks away, Claire was two. She came into our bedroom and looked rather quizzical about who this man was in her mother's bed.

I returned to Calgary in 1975 for the proper feasibility study. I went with Terry Lazenby, who was a wizard on the accounts and numbers. I was responsible for designing the mine. They had a massive piece of machinery, a vast bucket wheel excavator and an enormous dragline. It was so big it could have knocked out the West Alberta grid. In the end we told management that the project was uneconomic. It needed the world price of oil to be at least $30 a barrel – it was then around $10 – to make it work.

I did a year in Calgary, which was absolutely fabulous. I was looking at the Rocky Mountains and the beautiful blue sky from my office window. The people were wonderful. Ted Best the Head of BP Canada made our lives simple and enjoyable. For me, living in Canada was great fun. I learnt to ski. The family came too: Pam and Claire. Pam was pregnant for almost the entire time we were there. Kate was conceived and born in Canada. I had to drive across Calgary town at high speed to leave Claire with Terry Lazenby and his wife and then back to the Memorial Hospital to be there when Kate was born. I heard this cry. They told me to sit in the rocking chair. I was then given Kate to hold. It was brilliant.

Pam wanted to take our new daughter to show to our families back in England. She would need a passport.

I had been called back to London. I rang the British passport office. They could issue a passport but it would take time: there was a postal strike. And they did not know what the Canadian authorities would think about it. We contacted the Canadian authorities. They said Kate was entitled to a Canadian passport and this could be issued right away. But the British might not like it. We got her a Canadian passport. I remember holding this tiny bundle at the airport as we were leaving and the immigration officer saying to me, "She's okay, she is a Canadian. But you are an alien."

I was really sad to leave. We boarded a DC-8, a massive four-engine aircraft, which struggled and strained to get off the ground. As we took off, my eyes welled up at the thought of leaving this beautiful country. I almost left BP and stayed in Canada. There seemed to be opportunity everywhere. I had a skill that they needed. I suppose I was naive enough to think that I could get a job the next day. For the first time in my life I was wondering whether it was best for my family. I think if I had been on my own I might have taken another course. It was a difficult decision. You cannot go two ways. I do not have any regrets about taking that decision to come back to England rather than to stay in Calgary. Life would have been different.

Pam was focused on her family. That was a generation when a spouse, a wife invariably, supported the husband who was the breadwinner. That was what Pam did. She was an amazing corporate wife. She went everywhere, did everything and was very good socially with everybody. That really helped me and us enormously. She supported me right through my career with BP and after. It has really only in the last few years when she has asked me whether perhaps I should do a little bit less.

The role of spouse evolved. In the early times you just got on with it. One of the big characters in the company in the early days of building the Trans Alaska Pipeline was John Saint. He was one of a group of highly impressive technical managers who had come after BP acquired Trinidad Petroleum Development (TPD) in the fifties. I knew him in Glasgow with a mixture of Brits and Americans and American women fussing about the size of their tumble dryers and freezers. What are they all worrying about? he would say. Get the tent up and put the pegs in the ground. It was a completely different time. Expectations change in every generation. In my latter period in BP, I was spending time finding wives jobs in order

## 3. BRITISH PETROLEUM

to get the person that I wanted to go to Alaska, or wherever. Thankfully BP now has many more women working for the company.

Soon after my return I was asked to move into project management of the Sullom Voe Terminal on the Shetlands, the largest civil engineering project in Europe. We had 6,000 people working on the terminal. The pipeline was laid over 109 miles (175km). It was my first move out of pure engineering. Every other week I would fly to Scatsta airport in a Beechcraft King Air 200. It was a six-seater turbo prop with short take-off and landing. The pilot was ex-RAF and he would come in with maximum flaps and full throttle. But my boss as he saw the massive flare path at Heathrow said it was the best view of the Shetlands.

In the early days in the Shetlands I would stay in a hotel, which was cold and damp. The first time I drove there in the dark, the lights of the car suddenly disappeared. I braked sharply. I got out gingerly and could make out I had stopped just short of going into a huge dip.

My job was basically planning and finance. I was looking at ways to get financial management under control. I understood all the different parts of the engineering project. I asked sufficiently sensible questions to get everyone to understand the scope of what they were doing. It was huge. Nobody working on it had ever worked on anything of that size. As a result they could not actually get their heads around how big it was. It entailed the installation of a vast number of large gas compressors as well as the export terminals. Crude oil was brought in through the Ninian pipeline. Ninian was also a collector for other adjacent fields. We then exported crude in ships from the new terminal to the Rotterdam refineries and elsewhere.

Before I joined, every three months, another few hundred million went on the estimates of the costs. This must have been in part because people simply could not conceive of quite how enormous it was. When I was there, we got it to settle down to a $1.4 billion project. In the 1970s this was a huge exercise. However we did get it under control and we got it built.

Little did I realise that this was my last engineering job. It was important to step out of engineering. But I did not expect never to go back to engineering.

CHAPTER 4

# Time in the sun

IT WAS A conversation I had with a senior manager that gave an inkling of how things worked at BP. I had just finished one job. I was about to do something else that was very difficult. He told me I was a glutton for punishment. What I needed was a time in the sun. It is true: I have walked into some pretty difficult situations.

In 1979 the general manager of engineering asked me to go and see the chief executive of BP pipelines. Dale Lucas was a lovely Canadian. He told me there was a job that was really mostly about finance and tax planning. There might be tiny bit of engineering: putting in new pump stations to increase the capacity in the Trans Alaska Pipeline.

When I came back my boss asked me how the interview went. I told him I had a very nice chat but I could not think of a single reason why they would want me for this job. "No," he said, "you probably cannot. How fast can you get to San Francisco?" That was when I began to wonder what all this was about. I was not the only one. James Ross, who was the head of the North America regional directorate in London, remarked, "Oh my God, they've sent this bloody engineer. We'll never get another meaningful number out of them". This might not have been exactly time in the sun – but it was certainly a change of climate.

After that all my jobs were either at the corporate centre or doing business upstream. I never went downstream or into chemicals. I was always in Exploration and Production – the finding of crude oil and bringing it to the surface.

It was only later that I learnt how the system worked. I was still very young. The realisation eventually came that people on the 32nd floor were moving the pieces round on the chess board. They were seeing how

## 4. TIME IN THE SUN

to promote people they identified as having a future, by giving them broader training and stretching them. They were running the Individual Development Plan (IDP) scheme. Nobody knew at that time. All you knew was that every two years you were dropped into a job where you had no idea what to do. You were not equipped with the right skills. But you would do it. Then occasionally, you would go to the 32nd floor for lunch with a managing director.

They were right of course. I learnt how to make sure the figures were correct. Pipelines provided me with a route into accounting and finance, commerce and tax. It was truly my move away from pure engineering. Management realised that an engineer should not necessarily remain an engineer. They understood that an engineer might be able to do rather more than testing pipeline pressure. That is why they sent me off to do a commercial job.

Alaska – though I little grasped its importance at the time – was the great pivot point from the old BP to the new. The company had first explored for oil and found it in Iran – hence its original name as Anglo-Persian and from 1935 Anglo-Iranian Oil Company – then Iraq, Kuwait, Qatar and Abu Dhabi. For almost half a century BP flourished with this arrangement. Then as so often unstable geopolitics forced BP to reconsider its reliance on favourable geology. Two events in the 1950s spurred that rethinking of BP's global strategy. Mossadek's expropriation and nationalisation – however short-lived – of BP's assets in Iran; and the 1956 Suez crisis and ensuing war. The first underlined BP's over reliance on a single source of oil: at the time BP obtained three quarters of its oil from Iran. The second showed the vulnerability of shipping to political upheaval.

In the late 1950s BP took the strategic decision to turn its attention to the US. It was after all the largest consumer market for oil and oil products in the world. It also had some of the most developed oil provinces. Except one. The Lower 48 states were well covered. The one area that appealed to BP explorers was the untouched frontier lands of the far North-West: Alaska. And it was at exactly this time in 1957 that the US federal government decided to open up Alaska. The federal authorities were in charge because Alaska did not then exist as a state: it only achieved statehood in 1959. Exploration licences were issued. The industry flocked to acquire licenses, mainly for plots in the southern part of Alaska.

BP was little interested in that area. And – timing being everything – it

*15*

was a couple of years later that the authorities in the US held a second auction. This was for acreage on the northern coast of Alaska. It included territory that until then had been reserved as a future source of oil for the US navy. The acreage on offer was beyond the ridge of the Brooks Range that goes east to west, from the Canadian border to the Bering Sea. The North Slope runs down from the crest of the mountain range to the Beaufort Sea.

This was virgin territory in harsh and inhospitable terrain. High up inside the Arctic circle, it was a land where little or nothing grew. No trees. No shrubs. For much of the year, there was barely any sunlight; and in deep winter, the sun never went above the horizon. The permafrost extended over a thousand feet deep. This had big implications for drilling and for digging foundations. There were no roads. Supplies could only be delivered by sea during the small window in the summer when shipping could get through the pack ice. In a few months each year the sun never set. The tundra above the permafrost melted. Small flowers bloomed. The tundra became a mushy bog. Movement on land became difficult. Drilling was impossible. Only when the frost froze the ground hard again could heavy equipment be moved to the drilling sites, erected and set to work.

Alaska was a BP explorer's dream. It was dry, bitterly cold desert. And to make BP geologists feel even more at home, they identified in the foothills of the North Slope great folds of the earth's surface in whalebone structures or anticlines that in Iran proved to be the tell-tale signs of oil domes.

By 1960, BP had acquired 200,000 acres for exploration on the North Slope. The company set about drilling. Despite the promise, one well after another came up dry. It was very disappointing.

Then in the late sixties, another auction was held, for acreage on the coastal plain. When the next auction came, Atlantic and Richfield had merged by then into ARCO. It was ARCO together with Standard Oil of New Jersey (later to become Exxon) which were the first to strike oil in Prudhoe in early 1968. The three main companies had earlier agreed to pool resources. This included unitisation of the field. We were to have one port. One airport. One headquarters. And one pipeline to carry all their oil. For whatever challenges of drilling for oil in these inhospitable wastes, when they found it they would have to find a way to remove it.

## 4. TIME IN THE SUN

Shipping it was not feasible: for too much of the year access was not possible through the icepack. Later that year, BP joined the two US companies in forming the Trans Alaska Pipeline System (TAPS). The TAPS partners made a feasibility study. They would build an 800-mile pipeline from within the Arctic Circle up across the mountain ranges and over rivers and down to Valdez on the southern coast.

BP also bought up leases to as much acreage as it could: no company could have more than 300,000 and it had already used 200,000. ARCO and Standard Oil had obtained the choicest parts, the crest of the dome. BP settled for the periphery.

BP struck oil in March 1969. The find was a monster. BP estimated reserves in its share, about half of Prudhoe, were five billion barrels. Prudhoe was one of the biggest fields ever discovered, after the super giants in Saudi Arabia and Kuwait. BP which prided itself of the quality of its exploration and the low cost of its operations had done it again. It later calculated that its finding costs were 30 cents a barrel, comparable to the 28 cents in the Middle East.

The other issue BP had was to find a way of using the crude oil. It needed an arrangement with an existing US company. It found this in Standard Oil of Ohio. Sohio refined and marketed oil mainly in Ohio. But it had no exploration or development of its own since Rockefeller's Standard Oil empire was broken up by the 1911 US Supreme Court Anti-Trust ruling. Sohio had what BP wanted; and furthermore, merging with a US company made BP feel more acceptable in US eyes. The two companies complemented each other. With this arrangement, announced in June 1969, BP established a major presence in the United States. BP had two people on the board of Sohio from 1970.

BP started with acquiring 25% of Sohio stock, in exchange for its production from Prudhoe Bay. BP's shareholding would grow in step with rises in production from Prudhoe Bay. BP needed to take direct interest to relieve financial pressure on Sohio. When production rose to 600,000 bpd BP's share increased to 54%. It did not take long. Sohio was also the largest shareholder in the Trans Alaska Pipeline System, with 33.34%. ARCO had 21%; Exxon 20%; and BP 15.84%. This was the New World I was about to enter.

CHAPTER 5

# Time in a Colder Climate

I ARRIVED JUST BEFORE Christmas 1979. It was twenty years since BP first started looking at Alaska and when it had acquired its first leases. It was another ten years before they struck oil. And another eight or so before the oil could flow. Many of those who first had the vision and the courage to establish that foothold in Alaska were no longer with the company to see the fruits of what they had sown. It was a lesson to me. Finding and developing an oil field is a long-term process.

The building of the pipeline had been held up for five years by two major issues: concern at the environmental impact the building of the pipeline might have on the natural wilderness and migrating caribou; and the demands of the indigenous peoples. The pipeline operating company brought in 500,000 tonnes of pipe from Japanese manufacturers. It sat there with all the equipment – diggers, cranes and so on – for five years while awaiting approvals. Then the Arab oil boycott over the 1973 war created shortages. Lines of drivers queuing for gasoline became a political embarrassment. President Nixon reacted by authorising the construction of the pipeline. The US administration aimed to achieve energy independence. Alaska was key to that objective. BP had similar aims.

The people who went to Alaska had to learn to build igloos and survive in extreme conditions. Survival training was a key part of the training. These real frontier guys were still around to talk to when I arrived. The pipeline was massive, the largest privately financed civil engineering project in the world at the time. A 48-inch diameter pipe snaked 800 miles or 1300 km from where the offshore oil was landed at Prudhoe Bay in the north all the way down to the Valdez terminal in the south. The

## 5. TIME IN A COLDER CLIMATE

construction began in mid-1974 and the first cargo of crude oil from Prudhoe Bay left the port of Valdez in August 1977.

BP had only about 25 people in the pipeline company. Most of them were accountants, plus a lawyer and me. The man I was to replace tried to show me how to use a rudimentary early computer system to work on the finances. It was not long before the bloody engineer did discover a leak in the accounts that the score of accountants had not detected. I found they had made a mistake with the investment tax credits. It saved us $60m. It was a single piece of luck, but it entailed big numbers.

Although I was employed principally on the finances, as an engineer I did also make frequent visits to the pipeline. I have been to every gravel landing strip all the way along the pipeline. During my time we built more pump stations in order to be able to deliver greater quantities of oil as production increased.

I went everywhere. I saw polar bears on the North Slope. I took a helicopter to Fairbanks on the pipeline. We often flew up to Deadhorse. Flying round Mount McKinley [since renamed Mount Denali] on a day when the sky was bright blue was quite extraordinary.

I went fishing. One time we flew up to a lake in a seaplane. We landed by a river running out of the lake. Our pilot was armed with a gun. We left our big igloo on the beach and we walked beside the river fishing. I did not catch anything. I was as bad a fisherman in Alaska as I had been in Essex. But I saw lots of bones of salmon, completely stripped by bears on the beach, hence the man with the gun. When we stopped fishing for lunch we walked back up to where our box was. There were huge claw holes in the box. It had been opened and the contents consumed by bears. I did not actually see a bear, but they said from the claw marks that they were not brown bears. They were rather more aggressive grizzly bears. I was unscathed by these great beasts but was eaten alive by the huge mosquitos that appear in the summer.

In Anchorage they had cross country skiing, floodlit at night. I was invited to take part by the wife of one of the senior BP employees in Alaska. She was mega fit. It was my introduction to this kind of skiing. It was incredibly difficult and tough. You needed to be in incredibly good shape. I came back absolutely exhausted.

The pipelines job also exposed me for the first time to the broader political and social environment in which we operated. From 1979 to

1981, I was part of the pipeline organisation, getting to know ARCO, Exxon, and Sohio. We held regular meetings of the Alyeska pipeline company, which operated the TAPS. I would fly from San Francisco into Seattle and then Air Alaska up to Anchorage where the headquarters were. The oil companies that owned the pipeline were being challenged over the tariffs we were charging for the transmission of the oil. The plaintiffs felt that the figure we cited as the cost of building the pipeline – $10bn, a huge amount in 1974 – was too high. It was repayment for the cost of the infrastructure that made up a huge part of the tariff agreed by the regulator charged to consumers. By lowering the agreed sum for the building of the pipeline they hoped to reduce the tariff paid for oil.

I got involved with legal. We had a wonderful lawyer. George Hagle was a really great guy. He had been to Yale and actually trained as an engineer. He was unforgettable. I would sometimes go into his office and find him lying on the floor. I do not believe he had any impediment. He just found it easier to think on the floor. He did not care about anything. He used those yellow legal note pads that I had never seen before. If we were flying to Washington, which we often were, I would already be on the plane ready for take-off when he skipped in 10 seconds before the door was closed. He just did not believe in wasting time. I learned a lot from him. We spent a huge amount of time in Washington negotiating with the regulators who were on the Hill. We failed. What I learnt is that you cannot just negotiate with the counterparty without carefully managing the context of people and politics. We had dealt solely with the regulator. We should not have been dealing with the regulator alone. We should have been dealing more with Congress, both the House and the Senate. But I was young and did not really consider a more effective strategy. One learns sometimes by not succeeding.

There was another big issue I had to deal with during this time. BP had acquired a majority of Standard Oil of Ohio in the 70s. Sohio still had the largest share in the Trans Alaska Pipeline. However there was a conflict of interest between us and Sohio over its policy towards Alaska. Our deal with Sohio was that our majority ownership would increase as production increased from Prudhoe Bay. Of course the production could not increase from Prudhoe unless you put in new pump stations into the Trans Alaska pipeline to take the oil away.

Although we owned a big bit of Sohio we did not behave as if we did.

## 5. TIME IN A COLDER CLIMATE

We behaved like they were another company. That was one of the problems that needed fixing. It got fixed in the end. Sohio would be arguing in every conceivable way possible that we should not build another pump station. They knew that any increase in production from Prudhoe would decrease their control of the company. I was arguing really strongly that the United States needed additional domestic production. I felt at the time that I was raising the stars and stripes, and acting more American than the Americans! At the time the US was importing oil. I was presenting the building of new pump stations as a patriotic duty, serving US national interests. It was not a ploy to increase BP's control of Sohio. However that was of course the result, after we agreed to build more pump stations.

Sitting with me as the BP member on the operating committee of the Alyeska (TAPS) operating company were some far more senior and illustrious executives: Lod Cook, who was then chief executive of ARCO and chairman of the operating committee, and a senior executive from Exxon. Despite their greater years and experience, I never felt in awe of them. I treated these grizzled old oilmen who had been in the business for years as equals, even though I had only been six years at BP. I played tennis with Lod Cook in Phoenix, Arizona. I do not play tennis very well. But I never felt I was the office boy fetching the coffee.

When Dale Lucas who had hired me left, BP put in someone from the downstream business. He clearly was not as accomplished as Dale. So if the head of BP America Alastair Manson, based in New York, wanted to know something about BP pipelines, he would ask me. I had frequent and fruitful dealings with Dave Allen, Alastair Manson's chief of staff. He was incredibly young but had an unbelievably wise head on his shoulders. I used to talk to him and get his help when I was in California and he was in New York. David was younger than me. He had a bigger brain than me. David always knew more than I did. He was a man of considerable intellect. He had read chemistry at Oxford and then done a doctorate. Our meeting was the start of a friendship that lasted and deepened over the next 35 years.

I spent a huge amount of time talking to him because he was more in my time zone than anybody in London. He would have only been three hours from me whereas London was eight. Alaska was another hour away from California.

We were making at $6 a barrel moving oil down the Trans Alaska

21

Pipeline. When the group chief financial officer realised quite how much, he decided it should be run from New York. We were after all a Fortune 500 number one company, even with only this tiny number of employees. As one of the underlings, I did what I was told and we moved to New York. Pam and I had to uproot ourselves from Walnut Creek in the East Bay, where I would travel in to San Francisco city centre by the BART (Bay Area Rapid Transit). We moved to Old Greenwich. This was lovely but very different culturally from the Californian environment.

In New York I also got to know Dave Allen face-to-face. And his family. His daughter was born in 1981, just as we left. However our relationship continued through his entire life. He was the go-to person if you had a really difficult problem that you wanted to fix. Or you wanted help to think through it. He was somebody who could figure out the wood from the trees on almost any subject that you cared to mention. His strength was really his ability to help you think through things, to find your way through a labyrinth of complexity and arrive at a simple conclusion. To any team he brought huge intellectual clarity. There are very few people who have everything. That is why teams matter. He was a very good team player and essential to the proper functioning of any team. He made the rest of us look good as a result.

In New York I found myself catapulted into the more rarefied air of senior management. Pam and I were invited to dinner at Alastair Manson's beautiful apartment on East River. It was fantastic for us when we were so young. It was a very interesting period. It was also a bit intimidating. The guest of honour was the chairman. Sir David Steel always talked about the family. He used that word 'family' about BP. It was very much a paternalistic culture in those days, where senior management guided the careers of the junior staff. This constant change of job, this exposure to different areas, and gaining experience in different disciplines, was what the BP education was all about. And it continued for me over 31 years.

It was not all work. We chartered the odd boat in Long Island Sound. This was not the first time I had chartered boats. When I was working in San Francisco in 1979 to 1980, we first went to the Caribbean. The British Virgin Islands had almost nobody there. There were no navigation marks. No buoys. No moorings. No fancy equipment. It was absolutely glorious. Our children were quite little.

In the UK when I was racing, Claire used to come and read the echo

# OLVER & SONS,

GREEN BANK, FALMOUTH,

AND

LEMON STREET, TRURO,

## BUILDERS,

### Cabinet Makers, Upholsterers,

STATUARIES, SURVEYORS,

UNDERTAKERS,

PAPER HANGERS, PAINTERS & GLAZIERS,

### Auctioneers & Appraisers,

*Timber & General Merchants.*

Government Contractors.

**BUILDING MATERIALS OF EVERY DESCRIPTION CONSTANTLY ON SALE.**

*Sawing, Planing, &c., done at their Steam Saw Mills.*

Agents for Croggon's Patent Felt.  Ritchie's Patent Cork Beds and Mattresses. Stone-Ware Glazed Drain Pipes.

ALSO, FOR THE

GLOBE INSURANCE COMPANY.

1. 'The Olvers were into everything' [page 3].

2. My father, in his captain's uniform, to my mother, Christmas 1942.

3. My mother, Christmas 1941, a wartime keepsake for my father at the front.

4. Post-war baby.

# They met at school

## OLVER — LARKIN

A COUPLE who first met at school at the age of 11 were married at St. Mary's Church, Shenfield, on Saturday.

They were Miss Pamela Kathleen Larkin, elder daughter of Mr. and Mrs. H. R. Larkin, of Shenfield Crescent, Shenfield, and Mr. Richard Olver, second son of Mr. and Mrs. G. Olver, of White Cottage, Silver Lane, Willingale.

The Rev. R. T. Shiells officiated.

The bride, who was given away by her father, wore a dress of silk organza with lace bodice and overskirt, and a train appliqued with lace. She carried a bouquet of white and lemon roses and stephanotis.

Bridesmaids were the bride's sister, Gillian Larkin, and a friend, Susan Turl. Pageboy was Gregory Hamilton. The bridesmaids wore dresses of emerald green shot silk, and Gregory wore navy trousers and a white blouse.

Mr. Michal Olver was best man to his brother.

After a reception for 85 guests at the Masonic Hall, Hutton, the couple left for their honeymoon in Guernsey, the bride travelling in a dress and coat of stone, lavender and white.

Mr. and Mrs. Olver will live in Highams Park.

OLVER — LARKIN
Photo: Lindrum Studios.

5. My first mention in a newspaper.

6. Three brothers: me, Michael and Tim.

7. All the family at English Harbour, Antigua.

8. With Kate and Claire after the investiture.

## 5. TIME IN A COLDER CLIMATE

sounder while eating Mars bars. She would have been only six or seven at the time. Later when I had big jobs at BP, by which time she would have been a teenager, she would take the helm while I was taking phone calls.

I went back to London in 1981 and two years later became divisional manager for new technology with responsibility for offshore, the Arctic and enhanced oil recovery (EOR). The production management team was led by Mike Unstead. Jim Buckee who I was to know in Canada was also part of the team. It was my first time working in BP Exploration. I look back and assume that whoever was keeping an eye on my career development on the 32nd floor was ticking one of those boxes.

As technical manager I was dealing mainly with EOR. We had secondary and tertiary recovery. After oil came up on its own, we used different techniques to recover more: first it was water flooding, to maintain the pressure; then it was surfactants, basically washing up liquid, to scrub the rocks of residual oil; then it was gas lift; and now it is fracking, this particularly for difficult reservoirs or good reservoirs later on in their life cycle. I began to understand something about production engineering, including well technology.

The job also entailed one of the more cutting-edge areas of the company: the Arctic engineering group. They were looking at the challenges of oil exploration and development off the Labrador coast with the hazard posed by large ice floes. We even hired someone from the British Antarctic Survey at Cambridge, an ice physicist, whom we called 'The Iceman'.

BP being BP however did not keep me there long.

CHAPTER 6

# *Further Education*

IN 1984, I WENT on the executive programme at the Darden School of the University of Virginia. This was phenomenal. Those identified as the brightest of the bright in the company were sent to Stanford. However the high fliers sometimes failed to take off or crashed and burned. As I was to show, not going to Stanford was not a barrier to greater success and reaching the heights. These executive programmes were part of the personal and professional development of future leaders and senior executives. Some were undoubtedly slow starters. All needed a level of intellectual ability. I felt you also had to have those people skills that are broadly bracketed under Emotional Intelligence - EQ. You needed empathy. To treat people in a civil manner. You needed to be able to listen. To know how to get people to think they got to the answer independently when actually you had been guiding them towards that objective. That was the magic of it.

There was one single exercise that was to be a pivotal point in my maturing as a business leader. We were given a business game that went on day and night for several days. We were divided up into teams and given a challenge, a problem to solve. We had to maximise a business algorithm about production, revenue and cash. It was clear that our objective was to end up with a company that was growing. We had to be able to manufacture the widgets to supply the demand. We had to generate revenue and not run out of cash while doing so. Our team could and would work 18 hours a day. Some of the other teams had people who were up all night, running around corridors, shouting and screaming. We had none of that.

Of course the monitors were not looking at whether or not we came up with the correct answer. Above all they were watching how we handled ourselves. It was not *what* we came up with; it was *how* we did, and *who* stood out. Our team was diverse. There were people from different countries, with different skills and qualifications. There were lots of Americans who had no concept of foreign exchange and currency fluctuations. What I tried to do was to work on people to create empathy so that individuals would do extraordinary things.

The learning that came from this exercise was really about leadership. Our team came out top. This was predicted by the psychologist who dropped into our room for probably no more than ten minutes. He asked us who was leading the team. I do not remember if I said I was leading or someone else spoke up to say I was. He asked me why I was leading. Because the team asked me to, I replied. He asked a few more perfunctory questions. Who was the chief financial officer? Who was the head of production? Who was doing advertising? Then he quickly left. We later discovered that he went off and wrote down his prediction on a piece of paper and placed it in an envelope. He predicted that we were going to win. In the feedback, the reason he gave was because I had been chosen by the others to be the leader. The others felt that it would work if I was their leader and helped them achieve their goal. At first I thought it was a joke.

That one game, played out over two or three days, provided me with the single most significant piece of learning in my personal development in business. I learnt that I was a leader and that others saw me as such. The psychologist and other monitors had identified that the way I behaved and my leadership skills were incredibly effective. What I realised was that to achieve success, it was not about hard things. It was actually about soft things. And this had the greatest impact on the bottom line. Bullying by contrast might sometimes have a short-term effect. But people can react badly to be being bullied which can reduce the effectiveness of the enterprise. A Chief Finance Officer at BP once told me he could not understand how I was so successful: I think that exercise provided the answer.

On completion of my executive programme in 1985, I came back to head office to become divisional manager of corporate planning. At that time, it was incredibly important. It was headed by John Buchanan who was a wonderful man, a tough New Zealander. He was a fine scientist. He studied chemistry at Auckland and did post-doctoral research at Oxford and Harvard. He had split corporate planning into two divisions.

I had economics and econometrics: i.e. the price of oil and gas. Chris Gibson-Smith was running the other half. We were accountable for drawing up the agenda for the Monday meeting of the Managing Directors. This included country reviews. One of the countries that we reviewed was Italy. As a Young Turk from corporate planning, I attended the Managing Directors Monday meeting. The chairman at the time was Sir Peter Walters. He turned to me and said, "Dick, what's next?"

"Country review of Italy, chairman", I replied.

"Yes", he said. "What's next?"

So we never presented our review. Much later I was told that Sir Peter's belief was never invest in a country that started with an "I"!

I was also engaged on Project Winter: the attempt by the company to gain full control of Sohio. I was in charge of the slides on that Monday morning when we made that decision. We already owned the majority of the company, around 54%. We did have nominal control through the majority stake: we had failed to exercise it.

Sohio, in addition to its share in the Trans Alaska Pipeline, had assets in the Gulf of Mexico and the Lower 48. Even after BP acquired a minority stake in 1978 the management was still pouring money into dry wells in the Lower 48. Sohio had also gained notoriety for drilling the most expensive dry hole in history: over $1.5bn on a field at Mukluk in the Beaufort Sea 65 miles north-west of Prudhoe Bay. The geologists later found that Mukluk had been oil bearing, but the oil had seeped tens of millions of years ago to the Kuparuk field that was being successfully developed by ARCO.

This deference to Sohio should not have happened. Nobody did anything very much until Bob Horton and John Browne were put in as executives to sort out the mayhem in Sohio. I was never terribly comfortable with that. I had first met John Browne while I was in California. He was then doing the Sloan programme at Stanford. Bob and John were trying to improve the company before acquiring the minority share. They of course had an accountability to the Sohio shareholders, through the Sohio share price. But for the life of me, I do not know why Peter Walters as chairman did not just get us to buy the minority before we put John and Bob in. Why would you put two people in to increase the price and solve the problem when you knew you had to buy the minority at some point? That was always my concern about it. I felt we needed to prosecute

## 6. FURTHER EDUCATION

our strategy only after acquiring the minority. Inevitably they did start to sort out the problems at Sohio. So when we bought up the outstanding 45% minority share a year later it was at a higher price. We ended up paying more than we needed to.

Sohio was not the only acquisition we made. However I had other things on my mind.

CHAPTER 7

# *Family Worries*

It was a family issue that gave me great anxiety at this time. We nearly lost Claire. It was during that period when it was the fashion for young people to wear floppy sweaters. Even so she was obviously expanding. Pam saw there was an issue and took her to the doctor. She's pregnant, the doctor said. It was complete rubbish. She went for a scan which revealed she had a huge tumour in her ovary. The local consultant was preparing to perform a full hysterectomy on Claire. At 15. She would never be able to have children. She had already had the pre-med when the consultant told me she had been thinking about the procedure all morning and did not think she should do it. I wonder whether a male consultant would have been so open to a second opinion.

The consultant had been talking to London and Cambridge. She said there was a man in Cambridge, Ralph Robinson, the professor of obstetrics and gynaecology at Addenbrooke's, who wanted to talk to me. Later that night we spoke and he said he was pretty sure what it was. It was a very complex malignant tumour. We should do nothing yet. He wanted to find out whether it was surgically clear or not. He would want to have an oncologist alongside while he operated because, as he put it, these things in young people are incredibly ferocious. Rather than doing a total hysterectomy he removed one of the two ovaries, and a tumour the size of a rugby football.

Claire then had a programme of CT scans every six months. Less than three years later the CT scan showed expanded lymph nodes. The oncologist said not to leave it a moment longer. We had to act. With chemotherapy.

Professor Robinson was sceptical. He felt he had taken out all the cancerous tissue. He suggested they remove one of the lymph nodes and see what the issue was. Again he emphasised that with a young person, it could be anything. I told him to go ahead.

It was just before Claire's eighteenth birthday. The surgeon said he would be two or three hours. He showed me what he planned to do: go in from the front and take a lymph node out at the back from beside the aorta. After two or three hours, he emerged to inform me he would be another couple of hours. "It's tiger country", he declared. I paced the carpet for another couple of hours. He removed a couple of lymph nodes and sent them down to histology. He was right: there was no malignant growth.

When Claire came around, her first words were, "When am I going to the party?" Sure enough five days later, she was up and about with friends in a restaurant in Piccadilly celebrating her 18th birthday. The experiences made me lose my hair; she simply bounced back. I do not know how she did it. 18-year-olds are just extraordinary.

Professor Robinson was an amazing guy. He was right in what he told me on day one. It was exactly the sort of tumour that he said it was going to be. It was indeed very complicated. And he was right about the lymph nodes. He said we should stop doing the CT scans. Claire has not had a CT scan since. She became a doctor and a mother. She had twin boys, Alexander and Thomas, who were 5 lbs at birth and grew to be 6'2". Nine years later she had another boy, Oliver, who is also over six foot. It was a miracle.

At about the same time as Oliver was born, Kate had her first child, Amelia, who is our only granddaughter. Then 17 months later Kate had another child, Harry.

CHAPTER 8

# *Britoil*

Back in the UK, in 1988 we bought Britoil, the former state-owned North Sea exploration enterprise that had been privatised in 1982. Soon afterwards I was sent to run the gas business, including these new assets, as general manager Gas for BP Exploration Europe. We had promised the prime minister Margaret Thatcher that we would drill umpteen wells and that the mind of European management would be in Scotland. Britoil's head office was in St. Vincent Street in Glasgow. It was the most wonderful building. We called it a $30 a barrel building. There were gardens on every floor. Beautiful offices had patio doors that took you out into your own garden. The place was dripping in antique furniture, oil paintings and long case clocks. It also had the most wonderful wine cellar. It was installed by the chairman Sir Philip Shelbourne from a very well-known family: my elder brother was married into it for some time. After BP bought Britoil, the contents of the cellar ended up in Hill Street in Mayfair for the delectation of senior management.

Hill Street was the brainchild of Bob Horton. Somewhere for senior executives to stay in comfort when in London. Much later I was staying there one night and was asked what I wanted for dinner. "Something simple", I said. "A steak and a glass of wine". The wine was unusually good. I looked at the label. It was some claret of venerable age. I asked the lady waiting on me where she found it: "It was all on its own in the cellar". Thank you, Britoil.

Britoil brought a lot more than vintage wines. It had wonderful gas assets. Combined with BP's in the North Sea we had fabulous assets. We also had excellent people. Both BP and Britoil had some really good

## 8. BRITOIL

people, well experienced in the North Sea and in the business of producing gas, and also in selling gas. We created a fantastic team from the best of the best from both companies. We retained the right people. We were lucky to have the choice.

The main customer for our gas was British Gas. We negotiated to sell gas from the Bruce field. We had to have a purchase agreement before we could start the project. We basically had a contract for all the reserves. Take or pay was part of it. Price was the other part: how the price was fixed and indexed. We had such a strong position that on one occasion somebody called me from Marathon, asking me when he was going to be able to sell *his* gas. This triggered warning bells in my head. I did not think we should be seen to be in this dominant position by other companies. There was no competition at that time: LNG was not an option then. He should not have been asking me. He should have been asking British Gas. Even if they were not easy to deal with. But he obviously perceived that we were so influential. We were so large in the North Sea gas business at that time that if we decided to bring a project forward and sell the gas, he was not going to be able to - or at least that is what he must have been thinking to have made that call to me. I needed to talk to the lawyers. Our position was clear. We had done what we were told to by HMG when we bought Britoil. We had to sell certain assets and we had to drill umpteen wells. So there was no legal issue in the way the whole thing was set up.

It gives an idea of how long these projects take that it was not until 1990 that we started work on the £1.5bn Bruce gas project, in which BP had a 37% share. The first sales - which we had wrapped up years before - were not expected until 1993. We projected that the field would be producing 10% of the UK's gas needs.

I had a fantastic job. We were very lucky and successful. It was really the first real, important executive job I did. I could look back and say I put on $3 billion of value in those years 1988 to 1990. I was enjoying it in Glasgow, other than the seemingly horizontal rain, 300 days a year.

Then in 1990 Bob Horton asked me to be his bag carrier. He had just been made chief executive and chairman, succeeding Sir Peter Walters in March. I asked if I really had to do this. I was having so much fun building the gas business in Europe. He told me, No, of course you don't. John Browne told me not to be so bloody silly. Of course I had to do it. So I accepted the position. I became executive assistant to Bob, chief of staff

31

to his office, and head of strategy all at the same time. Bob was both the CEO and chairman, the two positions being combined in those days. David Simon was the chief operating officer. David and I have had laughs thirty years on about how I managed to survive, sitting between Bob and him.

Now as head of corporate strategy one of my responsibilities was to convene the Monday morning directors meeting. We did not all congregate in the boardroom. At the time Bob had people in the east and people in the west. Some people came to the boardroom. Others I had to get on the phone. The Monday morning meeting was not really a meeting of people. It was a meeting of voices – when they could be heard. In those days long before zoom or even a video link, when we tried to patch people through, phones could sound something like the alarm signal of a nuclear attack. I was the one who had to fix the technical glitches in a hurry while Bob was spitting blood.

It was a terrible two years for the company. We were not doing well, except for the advantage as the price of crude increased. It was a bad time for the entire industry. Saddam Hussein's invasion of Kuwait in August 1990 caused turmoil in the oil market. Until then crude oil had traded between $15 and $20 a barrel. The conflict drove it up to $40 a barrel, as the markets expected a threat to supplies. BP was not directly affected. It had no significant supply contracts with either Iraq or Kuwait.

During this time I was trying to help Bob to lead the company in a positive way and push through lots of change. Bob had a record of having turned around things in the chemicals business. He was very good at knowing when to fire people and how to reduce costs. He also could see that the company needed changing and changing radically. David also knew it needed changing. Changing the culture of BP from being like the civil service to a performance company. Mrs Thatcher had "privatised" BP in 1979, when she reduced the government's stake to below 50%. BP only become a fully quoted public company in 1987 when the government sold its remaining shareholding. We formally initiated that change programme in 1990.

Yet even before Project 1990, the new approach had already started in parts of BP Exploration. It was not as though there were no teams of people working in this way before 1990. The gas business was run nothing like the civil service. We had a small team and lots of assets. It was working fine. John Browne had become CEO of BP Exploration in 1989 and took a chainsaw to layers of management. John was a very good leader of exploration from 1989 to 1995. It was also when Dick Balzer was hired, initially as John's mentor and coach. Dick Balzer was a tough American from the Bronx. He had done a lot of work with GE. He was probably the world's best facilitator of meetings. He helped John hugely as we tried to find our way through to becoming an organisation focussed on performance. And we did find our way. The company had world class geologists, geophysicists, and engineers. We put them through business courses and we turned them into world class business people at the same time. It was an amazing period, at every level. It was amazing culturally. It was amazing financially.

We had a famous conference with the top 200 people of BP Exploration at the appropriately named Phoenix Hotel, in Phoenix, Arizona. There we laid out the strategy for BP to rise from the ashes. We were basically trying to figure out what to do. The big themes of the strategy for exploration were going for elephants and getting rid of the tail. In other words, aiming for a small number of giant fields, which would yield economies of scale; and selling off low-performing assets.

Phoenix was where we decided exactly how we were going to go about the change programme with the objective of creating a performance culture. What Dick Balzer explained would make a difference to performance was the way in which the strategy was executed. It was revolutionary. It was changing the culture of the firm. It was getting the human capital to work in a very different way from the 80s. We did it by education. Learning and development. Getting people to think through how to be business leaders as well as technical leaders. We did it by organisational development. People prefer to work in smaller units. They were liberated by the removal of layers of management. We basically created lots of little business units. We really had two layers: the BP Exploration executive committee and business units. We started to create chief executives of the business units. The person in charge was accountable. Part of that was processes. And the most important process, then, and perhaps even still now, was the quarterly performance review (QPR). Not only for the production or the exploration. But also for the financial results of that business unit and for safety.

At the same time we thought we needed to have some horizontal connectivity. People should talk to their peers or counterparts. Not only upwards to the executive committee. Or down to their own reports. That created a whole peer group process. Each business unit had its key performance indicators. Those KPIs were often measured against the KPIs in adjacent business units. This sparked some competition. Why is that person's safety record so much better than mine? What are they doing that we are not? We could perhaps learn from that. Why are their costs per barrel twice what mine are? People did things because they wanted to do things. Not merely following directives from on high. People saw how we could improve and they wanted to do that.

So having all the key performance indicators, and having the right key performance indicators, and then obviously, the right contracts for each of these business unit leaders. We did all these things. Rather than just being told that they had to do better. Organisational development was a very strong lever. We turned the organisation upside down every two or three years, just to keep it on its toes. It was continuous revolution. It was an organisational development lever. Later we realised we had too many business units. So we created strategic business units. Then we had different sorts of peer groups. Later still we would do performance management differently. We were constantly striving to improve the organisation, to deliver better performance.

The transformation was led by the Executive Committee of the time. John did a very, very good job throughout that time. He was fantastic. And he had a good team working to effect the transformation. It was a big change programme and it was an incredibly successful change programme.

The way I describe it is we lit 1000 fires. One of the fires we lit was under corporate planning. Corporate planning had been the place to go for those on the up. It was the university of BP. But corporate planning went. Fast track executives no longer trained centrally in one department. We sent them off as executive assistants to directors and other senior managers. They would shadow a top executive and learn at close hand how to run a business, how to act as a leader. We called these executive assistants "turtles" because they were fully immersed most of the time and seldom came up for air.

Furthermore 1990 marked the start of a radical transformation right across the company and from top to bottom and bottom to top. Before 1990, there were still echoes of the civil service. The company in general

## 8. BRITOIL

had huge amounts of complexity. For example, Authorisations for Expenditure (AFEs) required 14 signatures on them. Accountability was very unclear. In 1973, when I joined, I would go into the North Britannic headquarters building. People there talked about tea. The tea would come around at a particular time. How it was served depended on your level in the company. One biscuit or two. On a saucer or on a tray. So too with offices. I did not have an office at first. In offices, the size of the carpet depended on your level. Civil service culture extended to having long lunches with clients or customers, where a large amount of alcohol was consumed. As a result little happened in the afternoon until after tea.

Bob articulated very clearly his aims and aspirations. Our programme entailed changes in organisation and structures and also in the culture of the company. Our aim was to make BP the most successful oil company of the 1990s and beyond.

There were different ways of measuring how successful we were in realising that vision. Growth in the share value was one. Another the size of the dividend paid to shareholders. But these were not the only measures. Bob stated that BP must be the company that most people wanted to join. It should be the company with which customers and suppliers most wanted to do business. It should be a highly regarded company in every local community in which we operated.

Bob started the process but probably was not the person who could actually implement it. I spent those two years trying to implement change and stopping Bob doing anything what was not aligned with that necessary change. But he was not really the sort of person who could lead 100,000 people up the hill and create a new company.

At the same time the company was stagnating. It was producing $1 billion on $16 billion of capital employed. These sound ridiculously low numbers now. But some very senior man came to me for reassurance. He asked me if we were okay. He said we had made a billion dollars. I told him we were not okay. One billion dollars was not what we should have been making. We should have been making three billion.

We had at that time all sorts of disparate companies, all in the name of diversification. We had a coal company, a minerals company, a software company and a nutrition company. BP Nutrition had a range of products that were not typically part of the activities of an oil and gas company. We had salmon farms in Scotland and made the salmon feed. We made

*35*

animal feed for pigs; and cattle feed for veal production in the Netherlands. We expanded our European food business when we bought Nobre, the leading Portuguese charcuterie company. One feed factory was planned for Sardinia. However the plant never operated. Other diverse acquisitions included an animal feed company, Purina Mills, and the largest copper producer in the US, Kennicott.

Bob was decisive and grappled with some serious issues in the management of the company. But he was arguably his own worst enemy. Some people thought he was robust and aggressive. Outwardly he was. I saw him throw speeches at his speech writer in the car. He could talk to people in a way that often came across as offensive. Yet for all that he had a thin outer shell. On one occasion he went to talk to some staff. As soon as the meeting finished he asked me how he had done. I told him that I thought some things worked really well but that he might think next time about trying a different talk. He then walked back into his office and told his PA, "Dick says I need to go to charm school".

Bob went off on a spending spree. He bought the most beautiful sculptures to put around the BP headquarters building. At the same time his wife Sally was redoing Hill Street. All this was going on as if it was a new day. Bob once asked me where we should put the sculptures for maximum impact. "The cupboard, Bob," I told him. His reaction was incredibly negative. "Why?" he asked. "Because", I replied, "we're in terrible trouble". The oil price had plummeted after the 1991 Gulf War. The company was not doing well. Shell could buy us without going to the bank. The staff were worried. He could not be putting expensive sculptures around the building. "Dick's an old pessimist", he would say.

After two years I had probably the biggest break of my life. James Ross, a managing director, decided to go to Cable and Wireless. It very rarely happened that people left BP like that. This created a vacancy that set off a series of moves. Rodney Chase, head of the US, became managing director. The question arose, who could run the US business, particularly the upstream, the exploration and production division? My luck was being where I was. I ticked the main boxes: business school; and running the gas business successfully. But in addition I was constantly under the eye of the chairman and chief executive. I was offered the job in America, which I took in a flash. I got out not a moment too soon.

Only a few months later the main board was to meet in Alaska. As head

## 8. BRITOIL

of America, I was asked to go along. On the flight up I was grilled about Bob by a non-executive director, a retired senior British army officer, General Sir Jimmy Glover. He wanted to know what Bob was like. Jimmy was very able and was trying to get his ideas straight in his head. I was not party to what happened next: I was not in the room when the board decided to fire Bob and halve the dividend. We would have had to borrow the money to pay the full dividend. That would not have been very smart. When we halved the dividend, the stock price crashed. Fortunately, I was not caught in the tailwind. It could have gone another way. I could still have been trying to make Bob a better chairman and chief executive.

One of the results of the fall of Bob Horton was the separation of the roles of chairman and the chief executive. David Simon took over as CEO. He gathered his senior people back to London. No more would there be people dialling in for the Monday morning directors meeting. Senior executives would be based in London. Lord Ashburton of the Baring banking family became chairman. He was very down to earth despite his upmarket background. He was also very funny.

CHAPTER 9

# Back in the USA

My first move in the States was to relocate. Rodney had had his base in Cleveland, Ohio because that was the HQ of Sohio. I was to run Alaska and the Lower 48. Alaska was the big piece of business at the time. I thought the Gulf of Mexico could be an equally big business. The growth opportunity lay there. So I set up my base in Houston.

Before taking the job I had asked Pam what she thought about moving to Houston. She asked me how long each month I would be in Houston. I told her I would do one week a month in Houston, a week in Alaska, a week in London and a week somewhere else in the world. She said, no thanks, I am staying at home. She was right.

Those were the days of the Falcon 50. I lived in the air. To fly from Alaska to London we had to refuel in the high Arctic of Canada. On one of those refuelling stops a guy came aboard and he recognised me. This made me think that this was probably not the way to spend my life.

The local executive in charge of Gulf of Mexico was Bill Sears, a former Exxon man. He had been head of production operations for BP in Houston. Bill became in effect head of both exploration and production in 1992 when the head of exploration for the Gulf of Mexico left for Alaska. Bill was not an explorer. Bill did not seem very happy that his new boss was now in the same office. I quickly found out that Bill did not appear to be aligned with the new spirit of the company. Bill was very smart and very good at what he did. The trouble was he just did not want to move out of that zone. He was comfortable where he was and did not want to adapt. Bill told me they did not have any problems there. They were producing 18,000 barrels of oil a day. They did not ask London for any money. They were making a profit. I said, "That's interesting, Bill. Do you think that is what you are

## 9. BACK IN THE USA

supposed to be doing?" For of course I was fully immersed in the direction the company wished to take. We were especially keen on exploration, on finding more oil and gas, and not sitting on our hands. At the time exploration was potentially the biggest, most sexy bit of the whole company.

Bill's ambitions were limited and he appeared to be content with modest production ticking along. I needed to make changes but had to deal with him in a way that was politically possible. For political reasons, it was not possible just to remove Bill and press on. I was told it would not be appropriate for me to change him. I had to be patient. We had a plan. I basically changed all the people around and underneath Bill, all his direct reports. We also found a satisfactory outcome for Bill. He was promoted to run production operations for the whole of BP Exploration and Production, based in London, a very good job that suited his skills.

The man who had left for Alaska was Jack Golden. I wanted him back. I was soon to get him. It made a crucial difference. He more than any other person deserves the credit for the spectacular success BP was to have in the Gulf of Mexico.

Jack was a wonderful man with a very large intellect. He was an unlikely explorer. He grew up in a small town in Texas where educational facilities were limited. However his mother trained as a chemist and his father had done maths. Jack's academic career was in theoretical physics: he did a doctorate and then post-doctoral research, although his time was interrupted by service in the air force. He even worked on a project at Princeton set up by a small group of professors on nuclear fusion. He joined Shell where he knew enough to understand petrophysics and to be comfortable with the geologists. Then he joined Sohio.

In 1987 he had gone to Cleveland shortly after John Browne had sorted out Sohio and reorganised the US business. John appointed him head of exploration for the Gulf of Mexico. After looking at the inventory of the Gulf of Mexico, Jack told him there was nothing there to make a dent in Prudhoe Bay. To be successful we needed to enter the deep water. At that time we had neither the assets nor the capability. We considered first a company called Placid that was looking into the deep water. We lost out to Exxon. Then Jack contacted some of the Shell people he knew from his time there. It was a stroke of fortune. Shell were struggling at the time to finance a prospect in the deep water.

Shell allowed us to farm into the Mars project in December 1988. We had only 28.5% interest but this opened the way for us to gain greater understanding of the subsurface. It also gave us an opportunity to take a peek at Shell's technology. We did not have a lot of deep water technology or expertise at the time. We learned not only about the exploration – about finding the oil. More importantly we learned about deep water development and production. We then had to find staff to build a whole business unit to explore and develop and produce in the deep water for ourselves.

The Mars discovery well was drilled in 1989 and it became the biggest discovery in the Gulf of Mexico for 25 years. It gave us a huge leg up. The pattern that we could see developing was that the deeper water beyond the continental shelf had bigger and more promising prospects. This only encouraged us to go off on our own.

I brought in people who really helped me. They were the types who would tell me exactly what they thought and what needed to be done. Whether I liked it or not. That was what we did. When I arrived, we had the wrong strategy. It was about to change. Key of course was Jack.

John had already articulated the strategy. This had been endorsed by Bob Horton back in 1990. We would take a gamble on frontier areas, the world's largely untested geological basins. The risks were high but these areas offered the greatest reward if successful. And we were confident we were able to harness the latest technology to help find these great undiscovered fields beyond existing areas of exploration. Our aim was to lead the industry. Not merely in finding new reserves. But doing so at the lowest cost. Production as well as exploration would be at the lowest cost in the industry. It meant breaking out from Alaska and the North Sea, which accounted for over 80% of BP's reserves and production. We were looking to go big in the new frontiers.

I started talking to all the subsurface people. We realised there was a huge opportunity in the sub-salt in the Gulf of Mexico. I formed a team of people. I either promoted them or brought them in from elsewhere. They were already in the company doing different things in BP Exploration.

Jack was to become a great ally, supporter and inspiration for me. Jack had a deep knowledge and understanding of the subsurface. Not only did he understand the science; he understood the Key Performance Indicators. He was also very commercially astute. He would be the first to say a project would not work because it cost X dollars a barrel which was above an economic rate.

## 9. BACK IN THE USA

Jack put together a team that included Chris Wager, a former US Navy Seal, to hoover up as much acreage as possible. The usual approach was to lease a prospect. We cast the net much wider. We identified everywhere where it was possible there was an oil field. Then we placed the minimum bid on as many places as possible. It was like placing single chips on the roulette wheel. We spread our bets wider knowing that any that came in could pay handsomely. That strategy led to the acquisition of Thunder Horse, Mad Dog and Atlantis.

Then in 1993 we did a swap for some of Conoco's assets. We acquired their Milne Point field in Alaska. In exchange we ceded a chunk of the Amberjack deepwater field in the Gulf of Mexico and obtained from Conoco some acreage in the Gulf of Mexico that proved to be key.

The challenge we had in the deep-water was that the seismic signals got scrambled by the salt. The salt crust in some parts was a mile thick. We knew this would act as a trap on any oil below. The difficulty was getting an accurate seismic reading of what was below, because of the distortion from the salt layer. Explorers until then had relied heavily on seismic data: the bouncing of sound waves against the rocks deep below the surface to try to map the lay of the rocks. The geophysicists, whose job was to interpret the seismic data, were having difficulty. So within the team we listened increasingly to the geologists, who were trying to picture the rocks from the bottom up to see how molecules of oil might seep up beneath the salt crust. The geologists told us that you have to have a really mature understanding of the geology: the source rock and the migration path the oil might have taken. Relying on seismic data was insufficient and misleading.

There was lots of thinking going on with lots of extremely bright people, a combination of geologists, geophysicists and palaeontologists. How many millions of years ago had the different layers of rock been formed? What could have been the source of any oil? What was the age of the source rock? What were the potential migration paths of the oil because of the subsequent layers of rock? Critically of course, was there a reservoir, in other words some rocks with permeability, for the oil molecules to be able to pass through? And was there a seal, to trap oil within the reservoir so that it did not escape?

The explorers in the back room were scratching their heads about how to visualise the subsalt. The team included Jim Farnsworth and Barbara

Yilmaz. Barbara was not senior but she had been identified for fast track development. She had all these maps out, with coffee mugs upside down all over them to illustrate her projection of the rock structures. I probably understood a tenth of what they were saying. But the combination of geology and geophysics and some very bright people, with different skills and areas of expertise, actually cracked the issue of the sub-salt.

We developed this further over quite a long period, months and months of analysis of the subsurface. We reached the point that we could see that there were real possibilities. Once we were confident of our assessment of what lay beneath the salt crust, we set about picking up further acreage through additional leases.

The person I brought in to do this and commercial work was Ralph Alexander. He had trained as a nuclear scientist but he was very good at negotiating. Ralph not only understood the sub-surface: he was very commercial. People used to say to me that Ralph was a bit of a problem. He was in a sense. He would jab me in the ribs. But you need people close to you who will turn the problem completely upside down and have a different view. That was Ralph. He was part of the team and we ended up having all these exploration discoveries. Then there was the question of the drilling. By that stage we knew exactly where we wanted to drill the wells. Had we got the money to drill? We were coming out of 1992 and the near death of the company. We could not afford to shoulder all the costs ourselves.

John was chief executive of exploration. I used to talk to him ad nauseam in his afternoons and my mornings. I told him we needed to drill five wells. They would not be cheap. We were talking about deep wells in three, four, five, six thousand feet of water. They were also deep beneath the seabed and the mud line, because they were sub-salt. Some of them were high temperature and high pressure – as Macondo was to prove fatefully and fatally many years later. I told him, we needed to drill Mad Dog and Atlantis and several others. All supergiant fields today but then just ideas. John said that I would have to find the money. I told him that in that case I would have to farm down. John agreed.

I got hold of Phil Aiken. Phil was an Australian who was to work for BHP. We basically built his company. We farmed out to him so he had a big ownership. Not as big as us, but still a big ownership, on projects like Mad Dog, Atlantis, and Thunderhorse. We planned to drill all these deepwater wells. Obviously, not every well is successful. Success could be defined in different ways. For example the Neptune well which we drilled in 1995 was a big find – but we considered it too difficult and therefore too costly for us to develop. It was then developed by BHP and turned out to be smaller than the ones that followed. But Neptune was hugely important for testing our assumptions about the subsurface against the reality.

I spent those three years building the Gulf of Mexico into something extraordinary. From 18,000 barrels a day when I arrived to creating over the period between 1992 and 1995 the potential to run a company of about 500,000 barrels a day by 2005 without asking for any money. That was the plan when I left the Gulf of Mexico. Before I came, there had been little stability in our operations in the Gulf of Mexico. We had spent millions of dollars but had little to show for it. What I hope I provided was a steady hand after a period of turbulence, and commitment to a strategy that did not waver. We continued to fund projects until we made the big discoveries. It was to be a 10-year period of huge growth and high margin oil. It was fantastic. In the event we did not hit that target in 2005. But we were to get pretty close. However, I was not going to be there physically to see the results.

CHAPTER 10

# Above Ground Challenges

During the time I was jump-starting exploration in the Gulf of Mexico I was dealing with other issues. My responsibilities also lay in Latin America. We had a lot of American staff seconded to the asset in Cusiana. I went down to Colombia to see how they were doing. I took Pam with me because we needed to check that all the families were well. Colombia already by that time had strict security protocols in place. When we landed, we handed over our passports to be dealt with by somebody else. Cars appeared on the tarmac and whisked us away directly from the aircraft steps. We raced through town with escort vehicles fore and aft, stopping other vehicles at crossroads and roundabouts so that we could race through. When we went to bed, an armed guard kept watch outside the door.

Shortly after we arrived we had all the American expats and their wives to dinner. We were nearing the end of the meal when I felt a tap on my shoulder. I turned around and our ex-SAS security guy was standing there. He told me that when we finished dinner, we would not be going back to the hotel. I said that was fine and we would roll with the punches. After dinner we went back to the office and found out that our hotel had been bombed. The SAS guys had packed up Pam's underwear and put it in bags. They were ready to deliver it wherever we were going to sleep. We ended up sleeping in the apartment of one of the Americans.

I also was busy dealing with Alaska, mainly to do with the pipeline. This time the subject was safety rather than the tariff. Arguments were being heard when I was head of the US before the House Energy and Commerce Committee chaired by the very aggressive Congressman John Dingell. BP decided I should present our case. The others defending the

## 10. ABOVE GROUND CHALLENGES

case were Mike Bowlin of ARCO and Harry Longwell from Exxon. I underwent another huge learning process. It was a potential nightmare. I went to Alaska. There was a stack of lever archer files piled high on a desk. I read them all. I had the context from my earlier time dealing with the pipelines. Then I went to Washington. Our lawyers had constructed a courtroom in the basement to resemble the experience of being in front of the committee. We hired some experts from the Communications Council of America to coach me on making my presentation and how to answer difficult questions. The lawyers hired actors to play Dingell and other congressmen.

We asked Harry Longwell if he would like to use our courtroom for his own run-through. He came one day and then had a stand-up row with the actor playing Dingell and stormed out. Later he invited me to a meeting at Exxon's Washington offices at the Watergate Building. He was protected by a phalanx of lawyers. He asked me two questions.

Would I agree to Exxon and BP formulating our introductory remarks as one unified response?

No thanks, I told him. We did not have time for that.

He then asked how many lawyers we were taking to the hearing.

None, I told him. He looked white.

We decided that before the congressional committee I would use a board for slides and talk to the board. This required a lot of preparation. I spent the best part of a couple of weeks working on it. When the other two gave their presentations they merely read from prepared speeches. Congressmen knew they would receive printed copies so they ignored what was being said and chatted among themselves.

When I rose to speak everyone looked up. They might have been intrigued by the non-American accent. It also helped that I was addressing them, not reading to them from notes. Then when it came to questions, I followed the coaching I had been given. Give a straight answer. Follow up with evidence to support the answer. Repeat the straight answer. I believe the video of that day was later used by Communications Council of America for training purposes.

I had very different experience with the Senate Energy Committee. I was invited to give them a presentation on the energy industry, which before the days of renewables meant oil and gas. It was on one of their trips abroad. I flew directly from Deadhorse to Avignon. No one cared about the carbon footprint in those days. If you're the Energy Committee your priority was not the impact on the environment. They were more concerned about the US economy. It was a very long flight but it did not do me any harm. It did not do the company any harm either. I do not know why they asked BP to do it. They might have asked Exxon. But then I never felt Exxon did much outside Exxon.

They had gone with their wives and taken over a large section of the hotel. They invited me to dinner after my presentation. It is funny what one notices about people's behaviour when they are outside their familiar environment. I was struck by how they ate their desserts. The wives would each take a dessert and then pass them round so everybody tried everyone else's. They did not even buy the drinks from the hotel. They all came off the 747. They had tables set up in the corridors in the hotel, covered with different bottles of whiskey and other drinks. They were entirely self-sufficient in terms of alcohol. You can look back on that and say, those were the days when one did that kind of thing. Nowadays, post-Covid, we have all become accustomed to holding meetings remotely on zoom.

The governors and representatives of Alaska were hugely focussed on the future. I got to know in particular Tony Knowles who became governor in 1994. What he and the other representatives of the state wanted was hope. They knew that Prudhoe Bay would be yielding up its treasures for many years. They wanted assurances about their rosy future. They had already accrued a lot of money. This after all was a state when a communication from the taxman was not a bill but a cheque.

I dealt with Alaska over so much of my life. I was always looking to take Alaskan crude out of the United States. But the export of Alaskan crude was banned. Under law passed after the Arab oil embargo, it was seen as American oil for the American people. It was even more than that. Under the 1920 Merchant Marine Act (the Jones Act) you had to ship Alaskan crude out of Alaska on American ships which had American keels and American unionised crews on board. You had to land the crude on the continental United States, other than one of the US Virgin Islands that had a refinery. Not wishing to put up with the status quo I asked John Gore, head of BP's government and public affairs team in Washington, what it would take to change the law. He told me, you will never change the law. I told him we should have a go. And we did change it. In 1995, President Clinton lifted the ban on the export of oil from Alaska after

## 10. ABOVE GROUND CHALLENGES

22 years. It was a lesson to me. It was an example of persistence and perseverance. If you start something you have really got to keep on going irrespective of whether the odds are against you. It took a great deal of time on the Hill. talking to politicians and convincing senators and congressmen. It was the right thing to do. I did that in the Gulf of Mexico and I was to do that when I left BP.

After three years, I was recalled to London. I had lived in Glasgow, Calgary, San Francisco, New York and Houston. I have had a sort of love affair with North America. Many of the non-British people I worked with were from Canada and USA. Of course in the seventies I had been tempted to stay in Canada. I was never to live outside the UK again, though the United States was to remain a focus of my working life with BP and after.

What was done when I was physically running the US from Houston was the strategy, the science, the identification and leasing of the acreage and the farm out, which was in effect the financing. I would not be there for the drilling of the wells and the production that we were confident would follow. I was not going to remain in Houston to oversee these developments on the spot. Yet I would continue to guide the continued development of our Gulf of Mexico assets for the rest of my career at BP.

CHAPTER 11

# *Running the World*

THE LONDON I returned to in mid-1995 was very different. John Browne had taken over as CEO from Sir David Simon, who became chairman. Rodney Chase succeeded John as head of BP Exploration and I returned to London to became deputy chief executive of BP Exploration. This allowed me to continue my oversight of the United States which was the biggest opportunity for growth in the company at the time. I was to remain at BP Exploration, first as deputy head, then as chief executive, for the next seven and a half years.

Early in my time, I found myself seeking innovative ways to make it viable to develop a small but still important field in the North Sea. The Andrew Field had been discovered in 1974. It lay 140 miles east-north-east of Aberdeen. With estimated recoverable reserves of 100 m barrels of oil and 150 billion cubic feet of gas it was hardly a supergiant elephant but it was sizeable nonetheless. In the eighties the company had looked at ways to develop the field. But the collapse in oil prices meant that it was difficult to find an economic way to do so.

In those days they figured out what the reserves were and how many wells you would need and then what you would need on the top sides. They would then cost the whole thing. Often they would find out that it was not economic so you would not go ahead. I suggested they turn it round the other way. Start at the economics. Ask ourselves what capital we could spend in developing this field so that the company made a return on its investment. So that is what we did. Then we knew exactly how much could be spent on developing the field, on the wells, risers, jacket, and topsides.

That was when the first alliance project was conceived of. We had to design a project that would not spend more than the capital sum allocated.

## 11. RUNNING THE WORLD

The next question was how we were going to get it built without costs slipping. I do not claim credit for the idea. It was Bob Scott, who is no longer with us. He came up with a novel way of approaching development. The Andrew Field was developed because we found a way to develop it quicker and more cheaply than the industry norm. Otherwise, it would not have been.

The traditional way was for BP as operator and main contractor to subcontract different parts of the work. In the new arrangement BP remained operator but in a more collaborative arrangement with the other contractors. We devised a partnership model that we called an alliance. The main aim was to reduce development and capital costs. But it also entailed a cultural shift. We were all partners in the venture. We all agreed on a target price: overrunning that target would be felt by us all. Coming in below budget would result in a division of spoils. We would share in gains or jointly shoulder losses.

Building an offshore oilfield platform is a complex construction challenge at the best of times. We decided to bring most of the fabrication onshore and tow out the drilling and accommodation modules to be in effect bolted onto the jacket. This greatly reduced the cost of doing all the work at sea. We were able to control and reduce time spent and so costs without compromising on safety or quality. The partners were working *with* us rather than as contractors working *for* us. The great thing about an alliance is that all are for one and one for all. If somebody falls over or has a problem, everybody is going to suffer. So everybody goes to help.

In practice BP also was applying the flatter organisational model that it had already initiated as part of Project 1990. There were smaller teams, and little hierarchy.

Another change from the traditional model was that all the contractors were engaged from the outset. Brown and Root provided management support and engineering for the jacket, topsides and subsea infrastructure. Santa Fe was chosen to design the drilling module. Highlands Fabricators were responsible for the jacket and piloting. Trafalgar House, Saipem, Allseas and Emtunga were the other partners.

It faced early challenges. In 1994 with the drop in oil price, BP needed to reduce costs. Every contractor managed to make savings. The industry benchmark for the project was £450m. Our target was £373 m. When the

49

project was completed it came in £80m under budget – and six months ahead of schedule. This was the way to go. Little did I realise what a useful model this was to provide for my future life.

One time we were about to drill in the North Sea with Shell. Shell was the operator. I asked Ian Vann, who had been chief geologist and then head of international exploration, if the well was going to be good or dry. It was going to be dry, he replied. I asked him why on earth were we doing it then. Because we were being dragged along by Shell, he said. And he was right. It was dry.

Within two years of returning to London, my life was to change again.

CHAPTER 12

# Top Table

AT THE END of 1997 and beginning of 1998 my responsibilities took a double step change in quick succession. During 1997 I was being considered for the board of Reuters. Sir Christopher Hogg the Reuters chairman was very careful. This could be expected of him, as I came to realise. I was put through a series of interviews and discussions. Finally he offered me the place as a non-executive director. It was the first board I went on though only by a few days. I joined Reuters board on 12 December 1997; and was elevated to the BP board as chief executive of BP Exploration and managing director on 1 January 1998.

My initial thought about Reuters was how on earth was I going to add value to a company so different from my own? The company's business was not really about news: that has always been a small part of it. The main part of the business was providing and servicing the screens that relayed financial news and data. It was a services company to the financial services industry. After all, that is how Reuters started: with Paul Reuter using carrier pigeons to bring news of the Paris bourse after the 1848 year of revolutions.

It did not take me very long to realise I could add a huge amount. I gained considerable self-knowledge: that I did have transferable skills. What I rapidly found out was that what we had taught ourselves at BP was equally applicable elsewhere: performance management, for example, and organisational development. I would ask the Chief Executive about the company's performance management process. I became heavily engaged in governance, not in a dry sense, but really about the way the company worked, and how they actually created performance for the stockholder, or did not.

On the soft side, I learned more about people. There was a cadre of people at Reuters who were very able, particularly in the Humanities and Arts. There were very few engineers, mathematicians, or scientists at the top of the company. I quickly discovered what they were excellent at and what they perhaps were not excellent at. It was all part of lifelong learning. I learned about boards and saw what boards do and how governance worked in practice.

I got to know the people on the board, particularly Sir David Walker. He was a former Treasury official who became a top banker. The government sent him in to rescue the Johnson Matthey Bank after its collapse in the mid 1980s. He had joined the board of Reuters before me. He and I were often in the same place on issues around the board table.

I did realise I had something to offer Reuters. Fairly early on there was a meeting of the Reuters board in New York. For some reason, I arrived late. The other board members had in front of them folders with pictures of people. They were of people identified by headhunters being considered as candidates for chief executive officer. As I walked in, they were all open at a photo of Jeffrey Skilling, then CEO of Enron. Chris turned to me and said, "Page twelve, Dick, you'll have an opinion".

So I turned to page twelve and I said, "Yes, Chris. Yes. I do have an opinion. Probably best to turn the page. You won't like the culture. Enron is a house of cards".

In little over a year the whole edifice came tumbling down. Enron filed for bankruptcy. Skilling was later convicted of fraud and sentenced to 24 years. He was released from prison in 2019 after serving 12 years. We appointed Tom Glocer. He took up his post in July 2001. He was an excellent chief executive.

I never knew Skilling but I did meet his boss Ken Lay. I did not get anything negative from Ken Lay, who was later found dead. He seemed very charming and pleasant. I certainly did not divine that there was a problem with the company from meeting Ken Lay. But I did divine it from seeing what they were doing in places where we were doing business like Vietnam, the Middle East and the power sector.

I suppose it was lucky that I actually had been around in that industry. I had sat with the Minister of Energy in Qatar who talked about the lady from Enron, with the short skirts. He used to say he was not swayed by short-skirted diplomacy. We were always thinking about strategy at BP.

## 12. TOP TABLE

Enron appeared to have almost no capital expenditure but were making a lot of money. It was an interesting sort of business school concept of not having much and making a lot of money.

Elevation to the BP board was a pinnacle but also part of a more obvious progression. And of course in contrast to my non-executive directorship at Reuters I was an executive director who had already been with the company 24 years. The combination of the two board positions running in tandem gave me excellent experience from both sides of the table as it were, the non-executive outsider and the executive insider, as to how boards could be run.

The chairman of BP was Peter Sutherland. He had been a director from 1990 to 1993 and returned as a director in 1995. Peter succeeded David Simon in May 1997 after Tony Blair, newly elected prime minister, picked David to be minister for trade and competitiveness in Europe and gave him a seat in the House of Lords. Peter was chairman when I joined the board and was chairman when I left. Peter was a wonderful huge human being with the gift of the gab that came from being both Irish and a lawyer. He had had an extraordinary career. He was the youngest ever attorney general in Ireland. He served as a European commissioner for competition and education. As European commissioner he launched the Erasmus programme that funded students from one country to study in another. So many student relationships were formed in this way he was dubbed the father of a million babies.

I loved Peter. He was a wonderful guy. He had been very helpful to me as well. His performances at AGMs when confronted with sticky questions were masterful. He would gracefully give the questioner time to speak, let them put their case, and then answer that he respectfully disagreed. He took the sting out of the questions and the pressure off the executives very skilfully. At one AGM an activist stood up and asked a long, complicated and hostile question. There was a huge amount of tension as he was asking this very awkward question. It was one that would have been challenging to answer. The questioner then stated he had got into the meeting although he did not have a share. Quick as a flash, Peter said, I grant you absolution. The bubble burst and the hall erupted in laughter. The question was forgotten.

Somebody then asked a question about the mating habits of the North Alaska caribou herd. Peter pointed at me: it was a real hospital pass. I answered deadpan that we managed to allow them to pass across the pipeline and that we were not a hindrance to the migration and mating habits of the Alaskan herd.

I had a huge amount of time for Peter. Peter was a former rugby player – a prop forward no less – and he had a reputation for never being shy of a fight. He got things done. But he probably needed to change the BP board earlier.

Within months of my elevation to the board, BP made the move that was to be the largest corporate takeover in history. We announced the merger of BP with Chicago-based Amoco in August 1998; the Federal Trade Commission (FTC) approved it on 31 December. Amoco had not been our first choice: we had originally approached Mobil but they felt we were too different. I think too many of them were unsure they would fit in with a merged company. The Amoco deal was absolutely brilliant. The top half dozen people in BP were involved in all the planning and execution of the merger. We also had Bob Maguire, then at Morgan Stanley, working on it. A small group of us would be huddling in John's house in Chelsea. The amazing thing was, we actually said to each other in the end, that probably a hundred people knew and it did not leak. In fact, I did not say anything to Pam. Pam continued with her role at BP by going with Richard Paniguian, who was head of BP Shipping, to launch a ship in South Korea because I could not come with her. Then the following day we announced the Amoco deal.

We had no significant problems with the FTC. Amoco was the right thing to do. We also bought Amoco at the right time. There was a slump in prices: gas was down to $1.7 per mcf (million cubic feet) and oil was wobbling around $9 to $10 a barrel. Amoco gave us all sorts of synergies. As a result of the merger BP became the largest oil and gas producer and owner of reserves in the United States. We got some great assets. We were to benefit for a long time from their very talented people: among many others, Bob Dudley later became CEO and Lamar McKay became head of exploration and Deputy CEO of BP. They also had a lot of experience in Russia.

The challenge of any merger of two huge companies is managing the integration of two ways of thinking, two different organisations, two management and performance cultures. We asked the Amoco people to identify those they regarded as the top upwardly mobile people, those

## 12. TOP TABLE

who would be the most likely to have executive positions. The trouble was, 45 of them were not truly mobile: they did not even have passports. I was concerned early on that we might have been getting ahead of the law. That we were sailing too close to the wind. You have to be careful when you are a public limited company not to divulge information that you do not divulge to other stockholders. If something is not in the public domain you cannot tell just one shareholder. So we resorted to clean rooms. Communication was often made through lawyers. When the gun was fired, we were already at a place where we knew what the business units of the combined company would be. I had also, with the help of my team, identified who would be the chief executives of the different business units and the chief financial officers. In each case we wanted one from BP heritage and one from Amoco. It was crucial to have a fair balance in the top management of every business unit. I was focussed on who was going to run Indonesia, Alaska, South America, the Lower 48. We also achieved synergy, saving money, by stopping Amoco pouring money down dry holes. We did a huge amount of early work so that once we had FTC approval we were ready to go.

There was one brief period of tension. Rodney was appointed as head of exploration for the merged company. This was the job I had: he already been elevated to deputy chief executive. There was an uneasy standoff for 40 days until it was resolved.

We met for meetings with our counterparts at Amoco's expansive country estate in Wisconsin, Red Crown Lodge. Everyone arrived by private jet. The place was fitted out with lodges and a large conference centre. It seemed an extravagance and in time we sold it off. After that first meeting, I was due to fly back to Chicago with Peter Sutherland and then take the BA flight to London. However the weather was awful over Chicago and O'Hare was closed. I asked my PA in London to book a flight from anywhere on the east coast from where we could catch a BA flight. We flew into some dot of an airport on the east coast and went into the tiny BA lounge. There were five people sitting there: Peter knew all of them. Incredible.

The Amoco deal turned out to be huge. It transformed the company. It was not only the biggest corporate merger at the time. It was such a good fit it made the whole so much greater than the sum of its parts. It has really worked out and has been very good for BP. We acquired their prolific gas provinces in Trinidad and Egypt as well as acreage in the US.

Mike Bowlin, who I had known from Alaska, called us up when we were doing the Amoco deal and asked us if we would like to buy his company. We told him we had rather a lot on at the time but we should talk in six months or whenever the Amoco deal was concluded. In time we did indeed buy ARCO: it was a $26bn acquisition we probably should not have made.

I was sent back to the United States to give evidence to the Senate Energy and Natural Resources Committee over the ARCO deal. Presumably neither John nor Rodney wanted to appear themselves. The chair was an old friend: Frank Murkowski, who had been Senator for Alaska since 1981. He was related by marriage to John Gore. The committee members hated the idea of BP having so much power on the West Coast. The Senators were talking to the C-Span television cameras trying to reassure their constituents that the price of gasoline was not going to go up in California. They stirred up fears that this would happen if BP gained a dominant position by acquiring ARCO's assets in Prudhoe Bay. It was basically cast as an anti-trust issue.

In the end the Federal Trade Commission insisted that if we were going to do the deal, we had to sell ARCO's Alaskan assets. These were the jewels in ARCO's crown. They had other assets but the acreage in Alaska was why we bought the company. Now we were being told to dispose of them. It was a terrible time for a fire sale. The oil price had slumped to around $11 a barrel. We did not see it coming. We should never have done the deal if we had known we would have to dispose of such assets. We failed to heed the lesson we had from the TAPS tariff negotiations, that it was not simply a question of negotiating with the regulator or counter party. There were so many other political interests and lobbyists. Anyway, we did do the deal. Rodney was in charge of the sale and sold the assets to ConocoPhillips. Every cloud has a silver lining. I got to know Ryan Lance who is now CEO of ConocoPhillips and we stay connected to this day.

The ARCO executives were sitting pretty. They all had golden parachutes. They had contracts that awarded them huge payoffs if there was a change of control. So we lost most of their good people. This was very different from Amoco. Looking back, I think ARCO was a mistake. I blame myself as well. I was on the board. I think we were persuaded by the success of the Amoco deal which was so good that we accepted the opinions that we were receiving that we would not have a problem with the Federal Trade Commission.

BP led the way in terms of consolidation through takeover or merger in the oil industry. The basis of our great success was above all in our phenomenal prowess at exploration and the development of the fields we discovered. This was to provide the foundations for the company's extraordinary growth, during the time when I was head of E&P.

CHAPTER 13

# *Making Magic*

WHEN I STARTED as CEO of BP Exploration, Scott Nyquist the oil and gas consultant from McKinsey came to see me. He had watched how I operated in the U.S. The first thing he told me was that I could not carry on behaving in the way I did in America. It was one thing to be very hands-on in one area of the world. It would be impossible to act in the same way dealing with businesses across the world.

I did not agree with him. The way I lead is by connecting with people. That is what I did. It is what I have always done. That meant I did have to spread myself far and wide. I went all over the world, wherever we had people working for E&P. I held loads more town hall meetings with everybody from the bottom of the company to the top. I was basically making sure that people understood the strategy and the direction of the entire exploration business, and what they needed to do every day to make that happen. It was the only way I knew. To use a bit of intellect and a lot of emotional intelligence. It needed me to be physically around a lot. That meant being on and off planes. I lived on an aeroplane. I did townhalls from Anchorage to the top of a mountain in Papua New Guinea. Everybody knew me. They knew what I wanted.

As a result, if I had wanted another $100 million EBITDA by lunch-time I would have got it. People were prepared to go for it, because people around the world realised that I needed it. They all knew me and knew what I wanted and were willing to do it for me. My management, my leadership was more about carrots than sticks. It was an extraordinary period. That is why our executive coach Dick Balzer told me, "What you don't realise, Dick, is that they love you". Those were the words he used. I took these people on the climb up the mountain, and we climbed this mountain.

## 13. MAKING MAGIC

I used the image of the mountain in a November 2000 BP Exploration conference in Phoenix. I quoted from Nelson Mandela, who talked about reaching the peak of a mountain, and then looking forward to one peak after another stretching out in front. But rather than feeling daunted, we should look back a moment and see how far we had come, how high we had climbed, what we had achieved. We now had five companies where once there had been one: BP, Amoco, Arco, Vastar and Union Texas.

Merging five companies, with five different cultures, was unquestionably a challenge. We needed to create a period of stability. Departing from Mandela's mountain imagery, I used the language of the sea. We should be moving on an even keel, not yawing to left and right.

There were several messages I wanted to get across. First and foremost the question of safety. We were to remain intolerant of unsafe acts in our organisation. We introduced a simple fix. The overwhelming majority of workplace casualties resulted from traffic accidents. We made it compulsory for all employees when driving or being driven on company business to wear a seat belt. Buses we used would have to be fitted with seat belts. Any person who objected to the wearing of seat belts would be invited to seek employment elsewhere. When people now question BP's historic commitment to operational safety, I would simply point to the sharp fall of workplace accidents across the group. We were committed to STP: Safety, Teamwork and Production.

This was not merely paying lip service. It was not box ticking. It was for real. We had personal contracts to ensure safety performance was achieved. When I or other members of the executive committee went to sites, we would do safety audits. On a visit to the Gulf of Suez, I took hold of a technician stripping down a turbine on an offshore platform. He worked for GUPCO, the joint venture set up between the state-owned Egyptian General Petroleum Corporation and Amoco in the 1960s. He could not understand what I wanted: he thought I was asking him how long it was going to take and to hurry up so we could get production resumed. It was difficult to get over to him that my concern was safety, and to ensure he was taking the right measures not to expose himself to risk. We were trying to change the culture, and attitude towards safety, that might previously have been too lax. This total commitment to safety showed clear and rapid results: a dramatic fall in workplace accidents on my watch.

BUILDING BRIDGES

I sought, particularly with the newcomers with non-BP heritage, to show how we went about business. It was up to me and my leadership team to convey some key messages: that although we were bigger, we needed to create smallness to create success (the Business Unit for example). We aimed at success. That was our focus and priority. But without compromising on safety. And we expected individuals to show personal initiative. Ask not what the company could do for us, but what we could each do for the company. We were focussed on doubling production. That meant turning over every stone. Something magical was happening. We would have to look at every single well, whether operating or shut in, and ask what could be done better. It might have been shut in when the oil price was lower. Now the price of oil was different, did it make sense to think again?

Our brand was different. We were not risk averse. The question we should be asking ourselves was not why, but why not? What I found emerging from this contact with people was the amazing energy and sense of purpose that they showed. Because as leaders we talked so openly about what we wanted and how we wanted people to use the space we provided to perform, they performed brilliantly.

What Scott Nyquist was counselling was the best time management. I feel that with the training at the top of a company like BP, you are thinking about different things every day. You really had to be able to focus on whatever the issue was at any one moment. Deal with that then be able to turn suddenly and do something completely different but which required exactly the same amount of focus. So one minute it might be Angola and the next, Alaska. One minute it might be exploration, the next minute wells, and then safety. To deal with this constant changing of focus you have got to be able to change gear. One minute, you might be at the board. And the next, you might have to deal with an HR problem. It was great training.

Another counsellor I gained when I took over as head of BP exploration was Dick Balzer. He came alongside me as my executive coach, much more than a facilitator. He was very good. He often attended meetings of my executive committee. He was there every time I held a conference with the top 200 people in the company. He would help during the meetings. We would sit together at one of those round tables and he would pass me notes. He was quick and open with any comments. After one executive committee meeting, he asked me if I had seen Andy's reaction

## 13. MAKING MAGIC

to what I said. "What the bloody hell did you do that for?" he asked me. He was really quite tough. He could read what was going on with everybody in the room. He was very good at that. I think I learned from him how to do that to some extent. He was an important part of the journey of culture change, performance management and organisational change. This actually created the magic that we were able to work.

The oil business is not all about technology. It is also about people. The people who work for you. And the people you deal with. We talk about technical challenges. We showed for example in the Gulf of Mexico that with the right people working together, and the right attitude towards taking risk, we could surmount the most daunting challenges. But we also had to deal with what we called non-technical risks. That meant dealing with governments and regulators and state authorities. In short, people. There is an open question whether executives can be trained to be good with people. It is the same question about whether doctors can be taught to have a good bedside manner, or whether some have it and some do not.

As a company we further distinguished ourselves by our extraordinary organic growth. And nowhere more so than in the Gulf of Mexico. At the same time as we merging with Amoco, we were beginning to see the fruits of the change of strategy in the Gulf of Mexico we had implemented from 1992. We had the most phenomenal success rate. Overall we had one really super outcome about every three or four wells. In quick succession we struck three elephants, three giant fields: Mad Dog and Atlantis in 1998, and Thunder Horse the following year. This was the best performance in the Gulf of Mexico at the time. We had a success rate higher than anyone else in the Gulf of Mexico. Better than Shell, better than Exxon. BHP paid for the wells. Every single one of the wells. Exploration wells could be quite expensive, $100 million a well. This was a big game. We drilled all the wells. This enabled us to actually develop all these supergiant fields.

It is impossible to overstate the size and phenomenal scale of each of these discoveries. They were vindication of our strategy and the product of our inspired exploration teams. They were a game changer for the company. We booked more reserves than our production and grew the company.

All exploration businesses are basically just emptying tanks. You find a reservoir. It has a tank of oil. You have got so many reserves. You open the tap and you run it out. When you have a business like that, it has a natural decay. The natural depletion is usually about two or three per cent a year or more. Sometimes it is five per cent. So if you are going to grow by five per cent you have got to fill the hole first, and then you have got to grow by a further five per cent on top. No company does that in the exploration business. They did it inorganically by buying another company. Exxon did it by buying Mobil. Exxon has never done it organically. We did. We were the best at exploration. And in that five-year period, we were very good at it. We were booking twice the amount of reserves in a year than we were producing. Reserves meant we were committing forward money to their development. It was extraordinary. The reason why we were very good at it was people.

We did what great companies do, which is to invest in people. Not only on the road, doing the razzmatazz. But in senior management, at the executive committee level. We spent a huge amount of time making sure that we had got the right people in the right jobs. We also moved people so each individual could maximise that person's potential. That is very different from just leaving somebody, because they are very good at a job, to continue doing that job. That is not what we did. As I was to discover, that was to be a huge difference between BP and BAE. Because BAE did the latter and BP did the former. So the magic was created by a wide group of people. They were simply excellent at what they did. We all learnt through the whole period how to perform.

Dealing with the people who were running our businesses remained what I felt most important to achieve the performance we were capable of, even after the acquisition of new assets from the Amoco and ARCO deals. I still felt the need to go in person, perhaps even more so, to explain the company strategy to those who were newly incorporated within BP. One of those places was Trinidad. Trinidad had been important in the history of BP. But it became large again in the modern era after BP gained Amoco's offshore gas acreage through the merger. I went down to Trinidad for a QPR and reviewed everything the team were doing and talked to all the staff. When I left, I told them it was a very important piece of business. But they had too few Trinidadians in management. There were too many American expats who had been here a very long time. They should promote two Trinidadians and send two American expats to a BP-dominated asset to learn about the BP DNA. We had to put in place a programme of help and education for the local employees. That is what we did. It was not long before we had a Trinidadian running the Trinidad business. Whenever I visited I would meet the minister of energy. That would be the norm, even if the main point of the visit to places like Trinidad was to look at the operations. It would not look good for a senior executive not to meet the minister when on a visit. But these meetings helped me to understand what Trinidad wanted from our relationship and I could explain to the minister what BP was doing and why. Of course the government always wanted to maximise their margins. We shared that goal, as long as we also could do good business.

One of the major assets we acquired from the ARCO deal was located in the far reaches of Indonesia in West Papua, formerly Irian Jaya, on the island of New Guinea. Tangguh was one of the most promising natural gas fields in the world. The challenge however was that the field lay in the middle of a community; and that community's livelihood from shrimp fishing was threatened by our plans to develop the site. There were issues over the Indonesia army's practices: it had a reputation for human rights abuses. The local population had little confidence in any role the army would play in maintaining security. So in part in response to our experience with public opinion and media attention over Colombia, we decided to set up an independent panel to oversee BP's operations and consult with the local community, with NGOs, and with different arms of the government. We announced the plan to set up the Tangguh Independent Advisory Panel in 2002. Its members, all prominent statesmen and diplomats, had years of experience in dealing with some of the world's most intractable conflicts. It was chaired by US Senator George Mitchell. He had headed the talks that lead to the 1998 Good Friday Agreement that brought some degree of peace among the warring factions in Northern Ireland. His deputy was Lord Hannay. David Hannay was a cerebral former senior British diplomat who had spent years trying to find a solution, as yet without success, to the divided island of Cyprus. The TIAP issued its first report on 12 March 2003.

One place where BP had historic interests but was regarded as arrogant and hectoring was Abu Dhabi. Abu Dhabi was the only place in the Middle East and North Africa that did not nationalise all the assets of the foreign oil companies in the 1970s. Abu Dhabi gained independence from Britain in 1971 and in time reduced our stakes. But we still had concession agreements and could book the barrels we produced.

## BUILDING BRIDGES

I went to Abu Dhabi around the turn of the millennium where I wanted to meet Shaikh Muhammad bin Zayed, the third son of the ruler Shaikh Zayed. Though quite young, he was clearly the driving force for change. We knew that his favourite restaurant was the fish restaurant on the beach. So we invited him to have lunch with us. Everybody advised me he would not show up. I told them not to worry and that we would have lunch in any case. So we all went for lunch and sat at a huge table. There were lots of people in the restaurant. It was full.

He did show up, together with Khaldoon Khalifa Al-Mubarak, CEO of Mubadala, the state-owned holding company, on his arm. Muhammad bin Zayed started off expressing his view that BP was an arrogant company. BP people were all arrogant. They acted like colonialists as though Britain was still in charge. He seemed to have assumed we were all arrogant, lording it over them and telling them what we thought was best for them. However he found that neither I nor any of the BP staff were arrogant in the least. He visibly warmed and ended up talking about the world and all manner of issues. It was quite extraordinary.

Shaikh Muhammad stayed for most of the afternoon. He did not go. We were talking about the business and what needed to be done. All the other people in the restaurant had finished their lunch and gone. We alone were left at the table. Our guys could not believe it. The experience showed that you need to have the courtesy to demonstrate that you are interested in people and their country and their business. Later Mike Daly, the head of the business unit in the Gulf, was to establish an unusually close relationship with Shaikh Muhammad. They used to take long walks together. Shaikh Muhammad was always going on about education. He told Mike Daly that if BP had educated 20 nationals from the Emirates a year over the previous 50 years BP had been there it would have made a huge difference.

A touch of humility is seldom out of place. It was an approach that ensured we had a relationship in the years that followed after I had left BP. I was to value the insights Shaikh Muhammad gave me about regional politics. I had been in Abu Dhabi when it looked like there was going to be war on Iraq. It was a few months after the attack on the World Trade Center. US Vice President Dick Cheney was due to visit Muhammad bin Zayed in the following days, hoping to garner support for any American action. I asked Shaikh Muhammad what he was going to say to Cheney. He replied that he would tell Cheney that Saddam Hussein was a terrible

## 13. MAKING MAGIC

man but one should bear in mind that "the man behind the man could be worse than the man". Muhammad bin Zayed said they knew how bad Saddam was. At some point during the earlier 1990-1 conflict, the Iraqi embassy in Abu Dhabi was evacuated. Officials went into the embassy and found plans to pollute Abu Dhabi's water supply. Another thing he said he would tell Cheney was however bad Iraq and Saddam were, and Saddam in particular was a bad person, the bigger problem Cheney needed to sort out first was Palestine. How right that seems today.

I had presided over our success in the Gulf of Mexico. Now in London I was also driving exploration success finding supergiant fields around the world. One of these was Angola; another was Algeria. Both posed above ground challenges. Both countries had been wracked by civil war or internal conflict. These challenges needed addressing to ensure the safety of our operations.

In Angola our core activity was removing oil and gas to the highest standards of performance and creating energy. We were also nation building. As everywhere else we operated, we wanted to leave the place better than we found it. Angola had a lot of non-governmental organisations clearing mines strewn around during past wars. We were working in partnership with a Danish NGO that had a fantastic model. One person would go to a village with tiny amounts of money, which we funded. The individual would work with the village. He would get the villagers to build the school, dig the water wells and erect the lavatories. It was just extraordinary. I went into the hospital and was surprised that it was not a bit more high-tech. The Danish aid worker said that if we put a stainless-steel hospital in here, it would get trashed. It had to be what they do. He was really impressive.

There were concerns internally about working in Angola given its human rights record and corruption. Many of us wrestled with this, often uneasily. I still felt we could be a force for good in a country as poor as Angola. Oil was not often put in places which were shining beacons of liberal democracy. We had to ensure that in the way we did business and treated people we lived up to our own standards. Algeria was another country where there had been bloody internal conflict. And again, we felt we could contribute to the betterment of society in general by providing jobs and livelihoods and helping the country exploit its considerable resources of natural gas.

Our gas project in Algeria was deep in the desert. It was a tough place at that time. We went down with the British ambassador on BP's plane. On landing we got into the embassy Range Rover with the ambassador. I could tell that it was a bulletproof vehicle. When I tried to open or close the doors, they seemed to weigh a tonne. If anything were to happen, the ambassador told me, we were just to hit the ground. In front of and behind us were other Land Rovers with fully equipped SAS people. He dropped me at my office where we had a safe room. It had a huge door like a vault at the Bank of England. We were to go in there if there was a problem. There was a problem, a huge problem, after my time: a bloody attack in In Amenas in 2013.

CHAPTER 14

# BP Explorer

SOME OF THE places where I went to conduct QPRs were new to me. Others were not. I went to Vietnam for the first time in early 2001. I was on my way to Sydney where I was to join the *BP Explorer*, the Global Challenge boat, at the start of a leg of the round-the-world race. I went with John Minge, my executive assistant right through to when I left the company in 2004. He like all executive assistants was exposed to what it means to be a leader, morning to night, seven days a week. He later became the chairman of BP America. He was a lovely man and an excellent person. He was a real operator. In the North Sea, he had been in charge of offshore rigs: he knew about safety and his attitude helped me a lot. He knew what he was talking about.

I was slightly apprehensive going to Vietnam, travelling with an American executive assistant. I quickly realised I had no reason to be. The staff were absolutely charming. They were all young. There were a lot of women. They called it the American war, if they mentioned it at all. They were all born after it. There was absolutely zero problem with John, who had very good inter-personal skills anyway. They gave me some fabulous black and white pictures of Vietnam. And they gave me a model of the *BP Explorer* which they had made. I went to see the energy minister. His office asked me to wait a moment. Again, they were completely charming. They might have said they had no time that day but they did not. They could easily have put me off because President Vladimir Putin was making his first official visit to Hanoi.

My advice to the BP office when I left was to be patient. I knew they wanted to go fast. I loved the fact they wanted to. But they would not be able to go any faster than the Vietnamese authorities could handle. So they would have to pace themselves and not feel bad about it. They would get the approvals that they needed. We all had to work intensively with the authorities. And we had to do it at their pace. That is the advice I gave them: not to bang their heads against a brick wall. We did actually get the approvals in the end, for an offshore development pipeline and a power station. They were to be sold many years later to pay for the costs of Macondo. Vietnam was part of the then tail: it had not got big enough to be material.

I left Vietnam for Australia and *BP Explorer*. The Global Challenge had been set up by Chay Blyth, the round the world yachtsman, to pit identical boats sponsored and crewed by leading British companies. BP sponsored a boat twice: in 2000 and 2004. Pam named the boats in both cases. Each boat had a crew of eighteen with a professional skipper. The 2000 Challenge was shortly after the merger with Amoco and the purchase of ARCO, so we made sure we had people on board of BP, Amoco and ARCO heritage. It was just a small part of the integration, the cultural integration, of different parts of the company. We had also re-branded the company and the enormous spinnaker billowing out with the huge Helios sunflower was a magnificent sight. The Challenge was a really interesting exercise. There was a daily blog from the boat, and the blog scored a huge number of hits from around the world. I was set to do the Sydney to New Zealand leg. This was often called the executive leg, because it was not very long. Even so, I was just so busy I could not afford even to go on that. I was having dinner with Chay and I asked him why we could not make the final leg from La Rochelle to Southampton an executive leg so that we could share in the fun of an Ocean Race. We could have an extra 19th person on board every boat. Chay said we could not do that. However he must have slept on the idea. Because the next morning over breakfast he came and sat with me. He told me he had been thinking about what I had said. We were in charge. He then asked me if we were, to make sure. I told him we were. In which case he said we could rule that for the last leg we could have a 19th person on board. Each boat could choose who it wanted: a senior executive, someone from the media, or a seasoned sailor.

So that is what we did. I joined the *BP Explorer* at La Rochelle. It was not a picnic. We were really racing. *BP Explorer* was lying third at the start of that leg and we did not wish to slip back and lose a podium place.

## 14. BP EXPLORER

So it was an incredibly intense period of six days or so. I lost a huge amount of weight. It was extremely hard work. You slept four hours and worked for four hours. Every time you tacked, which we did a lot of because we were racing, we had to move all the sails from one side of the boat to the other. They were very heavy.

These 72-foot boats were stripped to the bare minimum. All excess weight was removed. They were racing boats. There was little luxury on board. We ate a lot of freeze-dried food that was rehydrated. When people ask me to tell them something that nobody knows about me, I say that I cooked for 19 people, including myself, at 45 degrees to the horizontal.

While we were at sea the organisers decided to extend the race. They held us back so we could arrive on the Saturday in Southampton for the television cameras. We ended up having a much longer race than planned. The race committee made us go round Wolf Rock halfway to the Isles of Scilly. We went backwards and forwards up and down the Western Approaches. Anyway, we ended up holding our position. Because that leg was more than 600 miles long, I qualified for membership – Chay Blyth proposed me – of the Royal Ocean Racing Club. I am still a member.

Our skipper on that boat was Mark Denton. He wrote about the experience for a Henley Management School MBA Text. It was aptly titled 'Inspiring Leadership; staying afloat in turbulent times' and was marketed as looking at the relationship between emotional intelligence and achieving sustained performance in the race. I wrote the foreword. After the race he did a lot of first line supervision training for BP: basically leadership training. It was about everything I believe in to achieve exceptional performance. Picking the right people to do a job, with different skills and personalities. Guiding them and leading them to work together to achieve outstanding results. On a boat or in a business. Sailing like business demands a high degree of preparation. Knowing where you are going and plotting a course. Being clear in goals so everyone knows what is expected of them. Coping when things go wrong. Dealing with difficult environmental challenges that you cannot control but which you have to sail through. And enjoying the journey.

CHAPTER 15

# *Reputation*

Back on dry land, I had work to do. I went back to Colombia where there were two big issues. One was technical: drilling. It was very difficult drilling, because the mountain was unstable. The rock was moving, not perceptibly, but enough so that we had a lot of stuck drilling strings.

The other big issue was far more well publicised: security. Security issues were huge. We had had people who had been seized. There was a Frenchman who for reasons best known to himself decided to go for a jog outside the camp perimeter fence, even though we were on a yellow warning. We were being accused of running paramilitary militias. It was not true. I had to refute stories about us paying paramilitaries and ransom for people who were kidnapped. They were without foundation. It was against the law to pay kidnappers to release those they had taken. We had firms like Control Risks who got most of them out. We never had a fatality until the Frenchman had a heart attack in captivity.

I was interviewed at length on Radio Four sitting in one of their radio taxis outside Britannic House. They grilled me. They suggested we had an army. I stated we had no army. I explained the role of the Colombian army outside the camp and our responsibility within the fence. Of course, we had really strict rules about going outside the fence.

Our experience in Colombia taught me another lesson. We were spending an awful lot of time on managing the company's reputation. That does not mean that we should only care about reputation in countries which had large and profitable assets. But it should have made us think that we should have been in Colombia only for good commercial reasons, with or without the problems with our reputation. It was not the Gulf of Mexico. Nor was it Alaska. It was a hell of a problem in terms of security.

## 15. REPUTATION

And it was a hell of a problem in terms of reputation, because of the narcotics trade. Production at Cusiana peaked at 310,000 bpd in 1998 - a not insignificant production - and was in decline after that.

Even before the collapse of the Soviet Union, the Azerbaijani government announced separate international tenders for licences for the exploration and development of the Azeri, Chirag, and Gunashli fields, a huge opportunity. Baku had been one of the first great oil capitals, dating back more than 150 years. In June 1991, we formed a consortium for the development of ACG. By 1992 we had set up an office in Baku.

The biggest challenge for Azerbaijan's bountiful oil - and gas, we were also to discover - was how to get it out. The country was landlocked. It had to go out by pipeline. The existing pipeline went through Russia. The aim of the Azeris and indeed the western investors was to avoid being subject to Russian control. Harry Longwell had another idea. Exxon had an 8% share of the ACG. They thought they could swap their oil out of Iran. That meant delivering Azeri oil to northern Iran in the Caspian and taking off equivalent oil from Iran's Persian Gulf ports. We said we could not do that because of US law, the Iran Libya Sanctions Act. We planned to build a pipeline to a terminal on Turkey's Mediterranean coast. I asked Harry whether Exxon wanted to be a partner in the Baku to Ceyhan pipeline. I told him the US government would not let them do anything to the south, i.e. Iran. Harry's reply has stuck in my mind. "US governments come and go," he said. "We're Exxon." ILSA was promulgated in 1996. Libya has been dropped from the sanctions regime. But the Iran Sanctions Act remains in place. Harry was right: there have been many US administrations since we spoke. He was also wrong: to date none has changed the opposition of the US to economic dealings with Iran.

At a subsequent meeting I told him we were going ahead with building the Baku to Ceyhan pipeline. I asked him how he was going to get his oil out. His hands gripped the edge of the desk, his knuckles white. He could not bring himself to say he was going to come with us. That was Exxon. They were bigger than everyone else and it was as though they felt they did not have to deal with governments and politics like smaller companies. Except in this case. In the end they did become minority shareholders in the pipeline. It was a massive engineering project.

In Azerbaijan, as in Angola, we were in the business of nation building. The place was so underdeveloped. We had to rebuild the steel fabrication yards. We took on many employees. We found there clever and talented and keen people but people who had been cut off from modern work practices during the Soviet period. We quickly discovered how their talent was not properly used. Once we found out that the person serving us a cup of tea was an engineer. We moved her off to work as an engineer.

CHAPTER 16

# *Peak Production*

ALL THESE ASSETS were to add to our growth. Perhaps I was just lucky but it was the best organic growth the company had seen previously or indeed since. I have a chart of production under the chief executives of the exploration company that shows this clearly. I was there when we increased production from two million barrels a day to nearly four million. Between 1997 and 2001, we actually achieved five per cent growth. It was absolutely remarkable, an outstanding performance by the team. How long could it continue?

When we all met for our annual BP Exploration leadership conference in June 2002, the mood was very upbeat. These conferences were very important for senior management. They provided the opportunity for us all running the businesses in the upstream to take stock of where we were. They enabled me and my executive committee to articulate clearly the strategy for the stream and how we planned to execute it. It offered the best environment to have the kinds of conversations that you can only really have in encounters face-to-face.

There was extraordinary energy in the room and around about it for the full four days we were together. My purpose was to say thank you to the scores of senior leaders who were there, from Alaska to Pakistan, from Angola to Azerbaijan, from the Gulf of Mexico to Abu Dhabi. The theme however was leadership and I wished to impart, I hope by example, my view of what that meant. But first of all I tried to express in two words a very simple idea, a very simple notion, of the culture we were trying to instil in the company, and which I believe we had already done so. Those words were Great Operator. BP had long been in the forefront in terms of exploration, of trusting its explorers to find oil and gas. But we now were striving to excel at developing those fields we discovered in the most efficient and profitable way: Great Operator. And to that I added a slight tweak: Our Way. Great Operator, Our Way.

As one of my executive committee Andy Inglis explained, we already had the best portfolio. Having created the best portfolio, we had to ensure that we matched it with the best productivity, which stemmed from being great operator. From Andy's perspective, in dealing with investor relations, it was hugely satisfying being able to stand before shareholders and tell them about the great assets the company had and the superb returns we were getting from the fields.

Many others in the room had their say: Jack Golden attributed the success of the upstream to the culture engendered in the individual business units that were given the tools and the space to thrive.

Ian Vann, that sage old geologist who looked like an Old Testament prophet, gave his own view of leadership: that it was a personal thing. Our styles were different. We did what worked for us. We spoke differently. We acted differently. Yet our objective was the same. We shared a deep belief in the linkage of strategy, performance, great operator, and delivery. And he said – and he had been around a long time – he had not seen that sense of common purpose ever before in the organisation. And it was a profound realisation that some of the pent-up energy and capability within the organisation was being released.

I have always emphasised how much I have benefitted from the coaching and mentoring and continual education I received at BP. Others too expressed the power of that approach. Ian Vann invoked the care and attention devoted to building a team, and then enhancing the team by being their coach, giving them the right experience and helping people be the thing they might be. As John told us, there is a difference between what individuals think they can do and what teams can do. That is what leaders do. They have to figure out what the team can do, and that is always greater than the sum of the individuals.

I for one felt very humble listening to the extraordinary stories of our leaders in Pakistan and Colombia dealing with the very different kinds of challenges they faced.

Bob Dudley, who came from Amoco, said it was with tremendous pride that he said he worked for BP. BP was the talk of the industry. He knew he worked for the company that had taken the leadership role about the

## 16. PEAK PRODUCTION

environment and also about transparency in doing business. This had actually changed the reputation of the industry. Writing this twenty years later it seems hard to imagine. We were a very different company from others. We set a trend in the way we did business.

As Bob spoke, I turned to Dick Balzer and asked if he agreed we were looking at a future CEO of BP.

Scott Urban, another of my great team who had come from Amoco, stated that the foundation of being a great operator had to be safety. This was the first zero that every one of us needed to focus on. Our company had to stand for zero compromise on safety on any BP site. This was not idle talk. He was able to cite the statistic: that in the first half of the year to date there had been zero days away from work owing to safety lapses.

That was then. Twenty years on, it is extraordinary and deeply concerning to see how BP fell from achieving an economic size similar to Shell to being valued at only one half of Shell. One well accident had cost half the value of a very big firm.

I picked up on what Bob had said. Being transparent in our dealings was key to the way we operated. It was important for the people in the room that we trusted each other. Trust was in short supply. Indeed, during the days we were there, MCI Worldcom revealed a multi-billion dollar hole in its accounts. There had been internal fraud on an enormous scale. The public could not trust such a company. And employees realised they could not trust each other.

Leadership is about direction. Clarity. We were clear about our target: to achieve five per cent increase in barrels produced. And we were clear about how to achieve this. We as leaders set boundaries. These were in effect the line between right and wrong, although we did not put it in those terms. It was our values. It was our ethics. It was the way we did things.

Then within those boundaries we created space. Space is created by having an ambition but setting the goal so people can win. That gives people space to act in the ways they feel inspired to act, within of course those boundaries.

Leadership is about support. It is about asking for help. And it is about giving others help. We need to do both of those things. In sum, for me leadership is about direction. Clarity. Boundaries. Space. Learning. Teaching. And magic. That is what truly makes the difference.

As I rounded up the conference I asked the question about how we were going to move forward. It might not be in ever increasing production. It might be less what we were achieving, but how, in terms of greater transparency. We might have reached a turning point. History would be the arbiter of that.

John had the final word. He congratulated everyone in the room on a job well done. And he spurred them on to reach greater heights. "As I keep saying to people, however good the past has been, the best, ladies and gentlemen, is yet to come."

They were stirring words. They were not to prove as prophetic as we might have hoped. For John had promised the market that we would continue to grow by 5% a year. He was not happy with that. In fact earlier he had decided that we could, indeed we should, grow at 7% a year. Now, anybody who understands the exploration business knows that you have to do a hell of a lot of hard work to stay flat. To grow at 7% was more than any major company had ever done ever in its existence. We had the most heated rows about this. John was insisting it had to be 7%. He was surrounded by people who did not dare challenge him. We eventually agreed on 5%. But even that could not go on forever.

In 2002, I was hearing from all my direct reports that even 5% was proving difficult. The people who were reporting to them were all saying the same. It was a question of physics - which John of all people, a physicist, would understand. There are only so many reserves in a company's inventory. They cannot be made any bigger. All the field managers were saying the same. Then at one point one of the deepwater platforms had a problem with its riser. They had to stop production while they fixed it. Events like that also put the brake on increased production.

From the ground up, people were saying the stretch target could not be met. We would be saying these things and nothing seemed to change his mind.

John persisted in saying this even when it became clear to me that this was unsustainable. I was the one who had to land the 5% growth. I was also the person who had to tell John he had to stop making promises to the market that we would be unable to deliver on.

There was one other person who also was not cowed by telling John how it was. John Buchanan was a fantastic CFO. He was not an accountant. He was a scientist. He was a brilliant guy. Other than me, he was probably the only person who would tell John which way up things were. He would give John the unvarnished truth. And at one famous meeting he did.

## 16. PEAK PRODUCTION

Interestingly, seven per cent growth is still etched in some people's minds outside the company. It was raised with me many years later in the Houston airport lounge by Julian Metherell, the Goldman Sachs banker who advised BP. I told him it was not seven per cent in the end, it was five.

The adjustment required after it became apparent we could not continue to grow at 5% was very difficult. Probably more difficult for John than many. I had told John at the Seville board meeting in September 2002 that we could not continue this extraordinary organic growth. I came back from that board meeting and told Andy Inglis that John would not listen to me. I did not think John knew how to deal with it. I told Andy to have a go with John. Andy after all was the numbers man. He was armed with the data. He got the same result. If John had said that these things happen, that we were only going to make 3% growth year on year, it would not have been so dramatic. But he would not do that. Then of course we had to tell the shareholders that after four or five years of growth we were not going to grow at the same level.

John then ordered a thorough review of all production. There was a period examining every large field. Some, like Mad Dog, had their recoverable reserves incorrectly reduced. In fact that field became even larger later on than any of us suspected at the time.

The Chief Executive Officer of BP exploration was the best job in the company. John had done it for a period. Rodney had done it for a short period. I did it for five years. It was brilliant. Then the right thing to do was to move on as, John Buchanan would say, the boys in short trousers needed to move up.

On 1 January 2003, Rodney left and I was made deputy chief executive, a role that never matched being head of BP Exploration. At the same time, Tony Hayward took over from me as head of upstream. He and John Manzoni (head of downstream: refining and marketing) were appointed to the board as managing directors, along with David Allen, head of strategy. Peter Sutherland asked me my view of having Dave Allen on the board. Peter and David were completely different. David was intellectually more able than anyone I ever met. He was on the same level of intellect as John. However he was not a forceful leader: he was not going to chop any heads off. I told Peter to take him. Because it was important to John. John wanted him. It was a team question, not an individual one.

Safety was not just about reducing, and we hoped, eliminating accidents at work. It was also about protecting those who worked for us against dangers from political developments or conflicts. We did operate in some difficult areas. I have mentioned Colombia and Algeria. In 2003, as the US and UK were poised to go to war in Iraq, I was faced with a decision about what to do about our staff in Kuwait. We had a few dozen people working on a technical services agreement in Kuwait. Kuwait of course was a southern neighbour of Iraq. And the impending 2003 action was in effect to address unfinished business from the 1991 war against Iraq. We could not know whether the Iraqis would respond by launching attacks on Kuwait. But if we pulled our people out this action could damage our relationship with the Kuwaitis. However I was not prepared to leave our staff in harm's way. I decided to pull everyone out. Better to make the wrong decision early than the right decision too late. In the end Kuwait was not attacked during the conflict. No one was hurt. Was I over cautious? Two things emerged. The Kuwaitis themselves did not in any sense feel let down. And the mainly American BP staff were appreciative of the decision to withdraw them. They felt it showed that the company really cared for its employees and their welfare.

It was a difficult time for me at BP. So much so that John Manzoni asked me why I did not leave. I told him I would choose my time. And that is what I did.

I realised that we only really needed one of the two of us. Either John Browne or me.

I was 57 and he was 56. At some point I asked him what he was going to do for the next three years. He said he was going to stay put. If John had decided to go at the top of his game, I would have become Chief Executive of BP. I was thinking what I was going to do if I was not going to become CEO of BP. I told him I would do anything I could to help but I was going to change my life.

I told the BP chairman. Peter was not happy because I was the insurance policy in case something happened to John. But I was desperate for a new challenge.

Obviously over 31 years one has ups and downs. However the whole learning experience was hugely positive. I had progressed from a civil engineer with a few skills to a leader of 18,000 in BP Exploration and nearly 100,000 in BP. It was a huge education for me. Literally, in the sense of passing through all the stage courses and business school in the US.

## 16. PEAK PRODUCTION

But also in a much wider sense. Learning about oneself and learning what one was good at and not so good at.

The decade from 1992 running America and then the entirety of BP Exploration was the most rewarding period. We created magic. I say "we" because of course my great learning before this successful decade was that the power of others was great and essential to getting superior performance. My role was merely in building those teams and in communicating continuously the direction, the strategy and my beliefs about how the performance should be achieved. Those people are too numerous to mention here but they created success in the Gulf of Mexico, Alaska, Angola, Algeria, Tangguh, Azerbaijan, Indonesia, Australia, Trinidad, the UK continental shelf and elsewhere. Many of those people we nurtured and supported through that decade went on to have distinguished positions elsewhere after they left BP, as I will illustrate later.

CHAPTER 17

# *BAE*

It all happened very quickly. I knew the BAE chairmanship was coming up: it was in the ether. So too was the chairmanship of another great engineering company, Rolls-Royce. The chairman there had had a stroke. I basically took the view that Rolls-Royce was a bit of a sewing machine. I was not correct, as history has shown. I wanted more of a challenge. I was certainly to get one. From early 2004, I began to meet and have contact with the top people in BAE. First, the chief executive Mike Turner. He came to see me at BP in the New Year. We had met each other through the new National Modern Apprenticeship Taskforce, the initiative of chancellor of the exchequer Gordon Brown. In our conversation I must have let drop that it was time for a change in my life. If John had decided to go, I would have been the happiest man on the globe to have the privilege of running BP. But it was not to be. So I needed to do something else. Whatever happened between us later, I am grateful that Mike Turner first introduced me to some of the BAE board. He heard what I said and I was asked to meet Sir Peter Mason. He was one of the non-executive directors at BAE: indeed he was the senior independent director. As chair of the nominations committee, he was tasked with finding a successor for Sir Dick Evans. Soon thereafter I met Michael Hartnall, another independent director. I had never met Peter Mason or Michael Hartnall before. But when my name came up, BAE under Peter's leadership appeared to do everything to accelerate the process of nominating me. It was as if their attitude was this was manna from heaven and they should get on and do it.

When I first met them I was in sales mode. I was keen to get the job and did not look too closely about what it might entail. If I had even seen the

## 17. BAE

press reports from the previous year that the Serious Fraud Office was looking at BAE, I soon forgot. The application process all worked smoothly. I was blinded perhaps by the idea that this was a different challenge. It was not an executive role: I did not expect it to be an executive role, although it turned out to become rather executive for other reasons. I was also reassured by the fact that I understood engineering, science, politics, and money. I had dealt with big money and big projects and governments. Project management was what I did. I had a lot of experience in all those things at BP. I thought therefore I would be able to cope with understanding this new company and what I would need to do.

At BP, I felt I was part of an industry that was a force for good and drove progress: our products enabled our customers to enjoy heat, light and mobility. At the same time we had a duty of stewardship: to leave the world in a better place than we found it. This might seem an impossible aspiration, especially in the light of current opposition to the entire fossil fuel industry. When I was making my pitch to BAE, I did not consider at that time what I thought about the products of the company itself. Nor the uses they might be put to by our customers, in a war for example. What would happen if the equipment we sold was used by the Saudi Arabians in Yemen? Should I be part of this? These were not thoughts or concerns I had. Perhaps it was because of my affection and respect for my father, and his wartime service. Above all, I believed in the company's role in providing the means for establishing and maintaining security in a turbulent world.

I had not at that time said anything about my soundings with BAE to my long-term personal assistant, Janet. I usually shared everything with her. But she did not have an inkling. I called her into my office and told her about my moving on. I asked her if she would come with me. She was visibly taken aback. She asked for time to think about it. She had been at BP a long time and had many friends there. The following day, I asked if she had reached a decision. She agreed to come.

I had also gone to John to let him know, before it came out in the press, that I was going to be chairman of BAE. The first words out of his mouth were that I would get a knighthood. I thought, how interesting. Why did he say that?

On 24 March 2004 BP announced that I was to leave the company. I would step down from the board on 1 July to take up the position of chairman of BAE Systems plc. I would however continue my association with BP. Peter and John had asked me if I would run BP's joint venture in Russia, TNK-BP, where I replaced Rodney Chase as deputy chairman. I was to do this for two years and three months – while also at BAE and on the board of Reuters.

I had not been a chairman before. I was entering not only a new industry but a new company and a new role. It was a new experience for the company too. The man I was to replace, Sir Dick Evans, had previously been chief executive. He knew the company and the company knew him. This had advantages; but I felt that it also had the potential to raise issues in terms of governance, specifically with regards to the independence of the chairman.

I had watched a number of chairmen in action from up close: Bob Horton, as his chief of staff when he was head of BP; and then Peter Sutherland when I was an executive on the board of BP; and of course my first board position as a non-executive director of Reuters. I learned a hell of a lot at Reuters. It was my apprenticeship at board level in a way. But it was more than that. I learned, first by observation then by practice, about process and how to run boards. It was fantastic to watch my chairman, Sir Chris Hogg, in action. He was very diligent. He would have a notebook and write notes throughout meetings. He was very rigorous in everything that he did. *The Times* described him as an "intimidating but civilised captain of industry who hired as well as he fired". That is what a chairman had to do. It is one of life's wonderful ironies that his daughter Cressida took my old job as Chair of BAE Systems at the AGM in early 2023. I had put more women on the board: now they were getting a woman chair.

I knew I needed to be absolutely clear in my own mind what my role should be at BAE to add value as chairman. First I had to have a very clear idea what the strategy of the company was or should be. My role and that of the board should be to help frame the strategy for the company.[1] We should then monitor the performance of the executive in their implementation of that agreed strategy. Then as chairman of the board I wanted to ensure that all members of the board were equally clear in their own minds what that strategy was so that they could fully support it.

A week after the announcement that I was to become chairman of BAE, I convened a meeting to discuss strategy with senior people from

## 17. BAE

McKinsey: Scott Nyquist, whom I knew well; the senior aerospace consultant John Dowdy; and Philip Rowland. The next day I met Andrew Davies, the group strategy director at BAE. Three months before I was to take charge, I was determined to initiate new thinking.

I consulted two investment bankers from Morgan Stanley: Jeremy Heywood, who had been Tony Blair's private secretary at No 10, and Simon Robey. Simon was to become an adviser to me. In time he started his own boutique bank, Warshaw Robey. BAE paid him a small retainer. He was around whenever anyone wanted him. Later I was to talk to Simon Robertson of Goldman Sachs. I little suspected that within months he was, like me, to take charge of one of Britain's celebrated manufacturing enterprises, when he became chairman of Rolls-Royce.

In the early days, I had talked to the non-executive directors of BAE, getting to know them. It soon became abundantly clear to me that some really did not appear to have a clue [2] what the company's strategy was. They certainly could not articulate it cogently. My assumption was that in the past that strategy had been worked up by the executive into its final form and then presented to the board to be rubber stamped. That was not really, in my opinion, the way to do it. Since the board had no input into the framing of the strategy, it scarcely owned the result.

That whole period between the announcement that I was leaving BP and actually taking over as chairman of BAE was fascinating. Although still at BP, I increasingly got to know senior BAE people. I had lunch with Dick Evans and dinner with Mike Turner. I also saw Peter Mason and key executives Alastair Imrie, who was head of HR, and Mark Ronald who was running BAE North America.

Even before I became chairman something happened that I felt was so serious that I needed to voice my displeasure. There were reports in the newspapers that BAE Systems was close to pulling out of the £3bn deal to build two aircraft carriers for the Royal Navy. BAE were in a dispute with the government after the company was rejected as lead contractor for the contract. It was widely surmised that the articles had been orchestrated from within BAE. Whatever the merits of the arguments, such public criticism of a government that was the main customer of the company posed commercial risks. I spoke to Dick Evans, telling him I had no right to say this since he was still chairman. However I would be sitting in his chair shortly. Had I already been sitting there I would have instructed the executive to cease and desist negotiating with Her Majesty's government through the pages of the press. And I would ask the cabinet secretary to instruct the Ministry of Defence equally not to negotiate through the press. Dick said he would talk to Mike Turner. I talked to Jonathan Powell, the Downing Street chief of staff, asking him to defuse the situation. I had met him through Nick Butler, BP senior executive for policy. Jonathan Powell was able, bright, personable and approachable. He did things when you asked him to. It became clear to me even before I joined the board that there was no love lost between the MoD and the company. I heard MoD people say, anyone but BAE is the answer. That was how it was.

The challenge was to determine how much the bad relationship was due to individuals and how much was a more deeply rooted issue within the company. My objective was to improve that relationship with the government. And it was not long before that relationship came under even greater strain.

BAE held their AGM on 5 May. I came to appreciate this was the best theatre in town. I went to the board meeting at eight in the morning before the AGM, even though I had not yet been appointed to the board: that took place on 17 May. I have no striking memories of going to a board meeting with Dick Evans in the chair.

In that period between the announcement of my appointment as chairman and my formally leaving BP and taking up the post on 1 July I also arranged to meet a number of government officials and ministers. I had not met most of them before my appointment. For BAE, the British government was crucial – and I quickly learnt quite how crucial they were and also how pivotal they could be in dealing with problems. It was natural that I should be introduced to those in government with whom the company had to have a relationship. These included (besides Jonathan Powell) Geoffrey Norris, Special Adviser in the Prime Minister's Policy Unit and at the Department for Business; Desmond Bowen, from the Ministry of Defence; Patricia Hewitt, secretary of state in the Department of Trade and Industry; and Geoff Hoon, defence secretary. I also made a call to Sir David Manning, the UK ambassador to Washington.

June 24 was a busy day: lunch with Sir Kevin Tebbit, permanent secretary at the ministry of defence; another meeting with Alastair Imrie to talk about personnel issues; and a board meeting to discuss the Saudi joint

## 17. BAE

venture. The most significant of those meetings, and the most ominous, was with Jack Straw, the foreign secretary, at the foreign office. We talked about how important the company was to the government and so on. Even though his ministry was not a customer like defence, as an MP for a North West constituency he was very supportive of BAE. He expressed forthright views on how difficult it was dealing with Mike Turner.[3] He was to say that "those who know him will know that he is no wilting violet". Many of the officials I spoke to in government bent my ear that the troubled relationship between BAE and the government was fundamentally connected to the difficult relations with one man: Mike Turner.[4]

BAE was not a state-owned enterprise. The government confirmed that. Lord Bach, parliamentary undersecretary for the MoD, had told the House of Lords a month before that "we are government; it is a private company. We cannot always expect to agree on everything". The government had no say in how the company was run, and who should run it. It had no business to tell us who should be chief executive. However it made little business sense to alienate the officials on whom the company depended for major contracts. It came down to knowing what was right and doing it irrespective of the risks.

I was due to start on 1 July but I had leave booked. And I had an appointment I had no intention of missing or postponing.

CHAPTER 18

# Taking the Helm

ON 1 JULY I was doing the theoretical part of my Yachtmaster qualification. The next day we held the naming ceremony for my new ocean-going cruiser, a Discovery 55. I called the boat *More Magic*, to recall those seven years of making magic at BP Exploration.

When I left BP, with Janet, she says she literally wheeled her chair across to Stirling Square in Carlton Gardens, the BAE head office just over the road from St James's Square.. Bill Wooley, my driver, came with us. The offices were so close, yet we were soon to realise there was a huge chasm between what we were leaving and what we were going to.

There was something odd about the new place. Something was not right about it. Janet in particular felt it was so different from the openness of BP. She felt she had gone back 20 years. Most people had been there forever. BP was already far more advanced in terms of diversity, trying to get more women in: more successful in the US than in Aberdeen but BP were working on it. At BP we were into openness and delegation of authority. There was also a lot more local hire in our operations abroad. That was not the only thing I found unsettling about the place. As I went in, I felt that something needed to be done here. I certainly did not like the sort of behaviour of some people particularly with the young women. I had a clear idea of what I wanted to do. I was less sure how I would achieve it.

BAE was a weird set-up. The chairman's office lay cheek by jowl with the executives. Normally the chairman's office is with the company secretary, away from the executives. Here we were next to the general counsel, a closeness that turned out later to be very useful. Steve Mogford the chief operating officer was opposite. Mike Turner was round the corner. You could sometimes hear what was being said.

9. Trans Alaska pipeline.

10. Horn Mountain production rig in the deepwater in the Gulf of Mexico.

11. Falcon 50 – my flying taxi [page 38].

12. Standard Oil of Ohio (Sohio) headquarters building in Cleveland [page 38].

13. Miked up.

14. Pam launching ship, Richard Paniguian in white gloves, the day of the Amoco deal 11 Aug 1998 [p54].

15. TNK-BP board.

16. Executive Committee bus. Lamar McKay driving; me and Janet Ling in the cab.

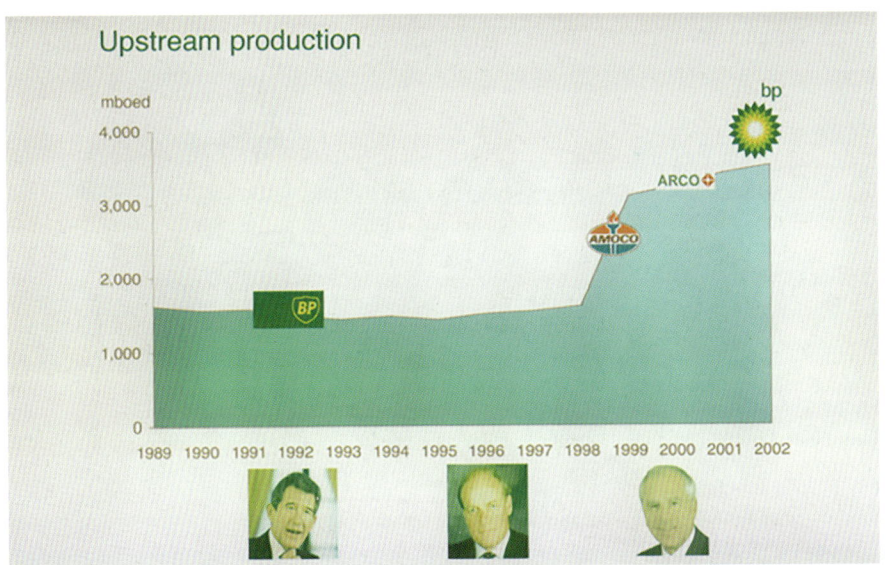

17. Upstream production under successive heads of BP Exploration: John Browne, Rodney Chase, me.

18. BP Exploration Exco *l to r*: Scott Urban, me, Ralph Alexander, Jack Golden, Tony Hayward.

19. The family on the slopes.

20. Pam, Claire and Kate on bow of Discovery 55 at naming ceremony at St Katharine Docks.

21. *More Magic*, a Discovery 55.

22. *Just Magic* – a J95 which I race in the Dartmouth area.

## 18. TAKING THE HELM

Neither I nor Janet ever had any sort of handover. This was not a case of Dick Evans sitting in an office for a few weeks and us down the corridor. Dick Evans went out one door and I went in the other. We walked in and he was gone.

In the days after becoming chairman I visited some of BAE's primary manufacturing and assembly sites to familiarise myself with what the company actually produced. I travelled to Wharton to see where the Typhoon multi-role fighter was assembled. My first site visit was the previous day, to Barrow-in-Furness where BAE was building Astute-class submarines. The next time I went, somebody came rushing up to tell me Camilla (who was to become Queen in 2022) was about to arrive. Would I go and welcome her to Barrow-in-Furness? So I nipped out to the airport to meet her when her helicopter landed. She was very easy to talk to. We discussed what she was going on do on her visit to the Royal Navy and BAE. We just sat on the edge of the helicopter with her big blonde hair everywhere.

Then a week after I took the helm, we held the session on strategy that I had been working on from the moment my appointment was announced. I used the annual planning session of the board as the excuse to introduce strategy. It was quite clear that there needed to be a lot more clarity. One of the major issues was whether we should do more in Europe. At the time we really did not do anything much in Europe, other than make parts of the Typhoon, known in Europe as Eurofighter. The question was whether we should continue to build a bigger business there or in the United States. Those were really the two directions. Even before my arrival there had been discussions about whether the company should merge with one of the larger European companies. There was always the debate about joining with EADS, Europe's largest defence company.

I proposed we set up two different teams, each led by a BAE person. We called them the red team and the blue team. One would have help from Goldman Sachs and McKinsey; the other from Morgan Stanley and McKinsey. One would seek to convince the board to invest in Europe. The other would try to convince the board that the strategic future of the company lay in the United States. These two teams went off and both produced really high-quality pieces of work. They then came back to make presentations to the board. But not in the board room. I did not want them all sitting round a large table. We went off-site, to Pennyhill

Park in Surrey. I had people sitting around small round tables, to provoke a conversation. I told the executive their job was to ask lots of difficult questions. This would help the non-executives understand what was being said. We had a whole day of these two teams.

Of course I had a firm idea of what I hoped the board and the executive would agree was the strategic priority. If you are chairman, the last thing to do is behave as if you are an executive and give the right answer. In my opinion, the best kind of chairman will walk into the room, know in the back of the head what the right answer is, but allow the room to reach that conclusion. They have really got to debate the issue and think about it and come to the right conclusion.

There were two major outcomes. The first was that we should continue to invest heavily and have a bias to invest in the United States. The second outcome was the extremely enthusiastic feedback to me from non-executive directors. It was the first time they had been to such an interactive, engaging discussion about what the company was doing. They learned a lot about the direction the company was taking. For the first time they felt they had a proper discussion with the executive. This might not have been quite what the executive wanted to happen. It depended on whether it was better to have a board that was helping, challenging, asking questions of the executive; or whether they wanted to throw a polished diamond over the wall and have holy water spread on it.

I felt I had put down a marker from the outset. It would not be long before the company faced a serious test. It was a test that would also bring to the fore the very shortcomings in the governance of the company that I was seeking to address.

I needed to learn how to become a chairman and learn quickly. It was quite different from my previous executive role at BP. Now I was on my own. That was how it felt. What I realised very quickly was that a chairman really has no power in himself just because he is chairman. You have to have a strong board of directors who make the right decisions on important issues and support you. Then you might have a lot of power.

So the first thing that I knew I had to do was to change the board. I started with those I could change, the non-executives, other than Michael Hartnall and Peter Mason. It is not something you can do quickly but it is hugely helped by the governance rules in the revised Combined Code in the United Kingdom, published in July 2003. Under the code of governance, non-executives were usually appointed for a term of three years renewable for another three years. Then after six years a very detailed review of how well an independent director was doing could allow him or her to extend their term to nine years. This could be further extended year by year, but only if very powerful arguments were made: otherwise people have to retire at nine years. This was to ensure they remained independent.

The Combined Code on governance of public corporations further stipulated that the Board should include a balance of executive and non-executive directors. At least half the board, excluding the chairman, should comprise independent non-executive directors. The board under Dick Evans had 13 directors of whom seven were non-executive. However Lord Hesketh had been a director of the company for 11 years – which under the guidance of the Combined Code rendered him not independent. The board was therefore non-compliant. He was accordingly the first of the non-executive directors asked to step down.[5]

Even before that, I began instituting what I regarded as world class governance. This included ensuring non-executive directors were having conversations without any of the company executives present. These are sometimes called Executive Sessions, a misnomer since they were by definition *non*-executive sessions. The purpose of these sessions was to provide an opportunity for non-executives to express any concerns they might have about the company or the executive. There might be thoughts about succession planning. It was right and proper to hold these meetings. It just had not happened at BAE before because the former chairman was in effect a product of the executive.

We did of course have a unitary board. But this did not preclude the need, indeed the requirement, for non-executive directors who were independent. Those independent directors had a common purpose: the success of the enterprise. Part of that was to make sure that the company was doing the right things and had the right strategy. The knowledge that I was for lots of change was communicated to the CEO by one or more non-executive directors after these meetings of the non-executives alone. These meetings were also to give space and time to non-execs to have a conversation about the company without having to be careful about what they said. At least in principle. Because I began to suspect that not all NEDs might have respected the confidentiality of what was discussed.

CHAPTER 19

# Bolt from the Blue

THERE HAD BEEN rumblings but in early November 2004 we learnt that the Serious Fraud Office was launching an inquiry into the company's business with Saudi Arabia, specifically looking at allegations of corrupting foreign officials. I had not been appointed to clean up BAE, but it was immediately clear that would be my main task.

I knew we had to address the allegations head on. Every bone in my body said we needed an independent review by a serious heavyweight about the ethical standards of our company. We could not get anywhere with the SFO inquiry but we could do our own review of our own performance.

The very serious legal and reputational implications of the SFO investigation were damaging enough to the company's prestige and standing. I had to persuade the board to accept what I felt to be the best way to respond: being pro-active rather than re-active.

I had experience of such an initiative. I was able to cite the way that BP headed off potential problems that could have arisen over the gas project in Tangguh. The Tangguh Independent Advisory Panel we set up helped BP develop a lucrative contract while also taking account of the concerns of local people about threats to their human rights. BP was a huge education really. Which is why so many BP senior people went on to such fantastic jobs after completing their BP careers. We knew how to get things done and done in the right way. By contrast when we hit this challenge at BAE it did not feel like anything was being done our way.

Accepting my proposal for an independent ethics review would be the behaviour of a twenty-first century company. In my eyes the essential elements of good corporate governance included having the right controls.

## 19. BOLT FROM THE BLUE

BAE had provided all employees with a single document, the Operational Framework. This laid out the standards of behaviour expected of them all, including business ethics. This was mandatory. The world had changed. The US Foreign Corrupt Practices Act had been promulgated in 1977. The OECD Anti-Bribery Convention came into force in 1999. If asked what the cause of the problem was, I would say it was not corruption. It was a failure of leadership.

The constraints on the industry had evolved. Long before my time, the thrust of the regulation in the UK was export control. Defence contractors were banned from selling to rogue states. Every measure was taken to ensure that weapons developed in the west did not fall into the hands of those inimical to western interests. Our record was good. No aircraft was flown to the other side. No nuclear submarine popped up in a hostile harbour. By contrast there exists a second-hand market for MiG fighter jets and the missiles strapped under their wings.

In previous times, a blind eye may have been turned to the way that some foreign contracts were secured. In BAE's case, the accusations of bribery and corruption were levelled at a tiny minority of the 100,000 employees. However all 100,000 employees had to face the constant criticism in the press. The tarnished reputation of BAE was a national embarrassment. Of the BAE employees over a third were in the United States. BAE Inc had long since been regulated by the Foreign Corrupt Practices act. This applied to US citizens and American companies. The vast majority of the remainder outside the US were engineers and technicians. They built aircraft and designed submarines. They were employed by a company that employed the highest number of engineers of any company in the UK. Those whose past practices were under scrutiny were associated with the international sales team and the senior executives who supervised them.

In the language of the oil industry, we had a burning platform. We needed to put the fires out. But I was intent on taking the opportunity to effect massive change in the business and the way the company operated. It was not just about being proper in our conduct of international sales. It was a wholesale rethink and reset of the way we worked. I came into a company where behaviour in the workplace belonged to another age. Many employees were ex-military; an overwhelming majority were male; staff were often treated brusquely.

I was determined to change the culture of the company, irrespective of how difficult it might be or what might or might not happen. It was basically the right thing to do.

First I needed the board on my side. If you as chairman do not have the support of the board, either you duck the issue or you change the board. A board that is thoughtful about everything and supports the chairman when the chairman is right. And a board that voices its independence when the chairman is wrong. I had taken that risk by accepting the job.

The executive considered that the board and the executive formed one team. That could make for an effective board if all were pulling in the same direction. But it did not make for a board that could control the executive if it was moving in the wrong direction. The whole point about having independent directors is that they should be independent. That is not how I felt that it was thought of at BAE.

Clearly I was proposing changes that might not have been quite what the team wanted. Some might have felt that no change was needed. It appeared that the executive decided that I was going to be a problem. If you were not a member of the team, you had better go. This is what happened to me.

Moving from being an executive at BP to chairman of BAE did not mean renouncing any role in the business side of the company. A balance was needed. My role was to provide leadership. One level was building relationships with foreign governments. Some people would say, we sold aeroplanes, tanks and ships. I used to say to them, no. We sell a relationship with Her Majesty's government. That was really important. It might be considered marketing or sales. Not that I felt like a marketer or a salesperson, but I dealt with many governments. For example, in Oman, where we used to have 70% market share, the Chief of the Defence staff, Jock Stirrup, flew BAE-built Jaguars with the head of the Omani air force. We were actually selling a relationship rather than an airplane.

Nine months after becoming chairman, I had flown to Singapore, a large potential market. It was a sobering experience. There I met Ho Ching, the Prime Minister's wife who ran Temasek, the state-owned investment company. I had gone to talk about aeronautics. All she wanted to talk about was oil and gas. She and the military there were telling me that the problem was that Britain had left east of Suez. If Britain had remained east of Suez, Singapore would not have had all this American

## 19. BOLT FROM THE BLUE

kit. They would have some of our kit. Ho Ching was in a position to know: she had previously been in charge of procurement at the Ministry of Defence.

A couple of months after this trip to the Far East, I was to get another clear message that my tenure as chairman was under threat from within. Fortunately I was forewarned.

CHAPTER 20

# Under Fire

I HAD JUST LANDED on a corporate jet in Southampton – I had been to see one of the non-executive directors Ulrich Cartellieri in Munich – and Pam picked me up. We got in the car and the phone rang. It was Roddy Kennedy. He was calling from Moscow, where he had been with John Browne meeting Vladimir Putin. They were trying to brief against me to the press, Roddy told me. The firm doing this was Bell Pottinger, whose co-founder Lord Bell was Mrs Thatcher's favourite PR man. It also did the public relations for the BAE Systems executive. Roddy was one of the wonderful people at BP looking out for me even after I had left BP. He said he had straightened it out but I needed to watch my back.

Two days later *The Sunday Times* ran an article[6] under the headline "BAE Systems chief executive tells chairman to back off". The article came out ten days before my first AGM as chairman. To expose such an open rift before such a public event when we would be on the podium together was unfortunate at best. The paper said we had fallen out over my involving myself in areas Mike Turner saw as his domain. In his view, the main role of a non-executive chairman was to manage the board and help the chief executive and be a team player.

The threat was clear. If I did not back down, I would be ousted. It was a massive personal crisis for me. It was reported that the senior independent director Sir Peter Mason was despatched to my office to read me the ultimatum. That is not quite how I remember things unfolded.

Having got wind of what might have been happening, I was ready. I knew that if and when the chief executive came into my office and said, the board would like you to resign, I would ask him what he was going to say to the stockholders when other non-executives would be going with me.

## 20. UNDER FIRE

In any event, I was not ousted. I stayed on and told the board I was intent on building a world class board. That would mean fewer executives on the board, and more non-executives on the board. I wanted Americans on the board to reflect our business in America. We had to ensure that all non-executive board members were indeed independent. That was the beginning of a fundamental change to the board and ultimately to the way the company behaved.

In the meantime, I continued promoting the company's interests at the highest level. In June 2005 I was in Washington, where opportunity was provided to talk to President George W Bush informally. Meetings could be staged at Ford's Theater. You could jostle your way to the front to have a quiet word with the president. As BAE was the fifth largest defence contractor to the US government, we had seats in the row behind him and his wife. Before the performance we could mill around. I spoke to President Bush alone: he did not even have a minder. The UK was trying to secure a technology sharing treaty with the US. The specific issue for us was over the Joint Strike Fighter. We wanted to ensure we got the underlying technology of the JSF. It should not be for US eyes only. This was only a couple of years after Tony Blair had supported the US in its 2003 invasion of Iraq. We were telling the US they owed us for coming with them to Iraq. Bush was very helpful. His problem was the bureaucracy, the United States government.

I also spoke with Vice President Dick Cheney. I first met Cheney in Europe when he was at Halliburton, one of the top two service companies for the oil and gas industry in the world. He was a very big guy who had big views. BP was obviously a very important customer. He was the chairman and chief executive: we were not talking about Well 356 or anything like that. It was more about what was happening in the industry and the world. He was really good on all that.

When we met each other next each of us had different roles: he as vice president and me as chairman of BAE. I have never been into the president's office. So I do not know the process to get from the street to the Oval Office. But the process of getting from the street to the Vice President's office is pretty out of the ordinary. There was a lot of security and people. Finally I ended up with the great man. He was a man with huge experience of world affairs. He had been Secretary of Defense under President George H Bush during the first Gulf war (1990-1). He was now Vice President to

President George W Bush. I repeated that we were the fifth largest defence contractor to the United States government. There was the issue of the JSF. I asked whether, and the extent to which, the United Kingdom would be able to obtain the source code and therefore be able to do upgrades and maintenance. Or would it remain for US eyes only? I had the conversation with him. I had the conversation with George Bush. I had to push on every door.

The UK government was also lobbying hard to obtain technology transfer. In October 2005 the House of Commons select committee on defence met to discuss carriers and the JSF. Its report noted that the head of the Air Force Jock Stirrup had stated "there is clearly a growing urgency in addressing technology access and the related ability of independent support of the aircraft".[7] This 'sovereign capability' – the ability of the UK to maintain these aircraft by themselves – became a huge issue in these parliamentary debates. Lord Drayson, minister for defence procurement, was holding out for the Memorandum of Understanding to resolve all these differences, due to be reached in December 2006. Lord Drayson later told the House of Lords that he had explained to his US opposite number the UK's requirement for appropriate assurances on information exchange. He conceded that matters relating to the Joint Strike Fighter were complex.

The select committee was assertive. "The procurement of the Joint Strike Fighter, a US-led programme", it concluded, "has also raised concerns about the UK's ability, in the future, to maintain and upgrade the aircraft independently of the US. To ensure this ability, the UK needs cast iron assurance from the US, its closest ally, that it will get all the information and technology it requires."

It never happened. We only got an export variant of the JSF. The Americans were very proprietorial. They closely guarded what they rightly regarded as state-of-the-art software. We were unable to fully maintain aircraft ourselves. Only American technicians could do so.

All the time I was working to create a world class board. I managed this through the nominations committee, of which I became chair in January 2005. It was the principal mechanism I could use. The code of governance stipulated that the nomination committee should evaluate the balance of skills, knowledge and experience on the board. That included having the best people available in the company as executive directors. But who were they? And how did we identify them?

Internally, I told the executive I really thought we needed an external review of our bench strength. I suggested they get somebody to do a review of the top 50 people in the company. This would help us get some idea about succession planning and who we needed to give what help to and so on. Because that is what one does in a twenty-first century company. I was told they already did proper assessments internally of senior staff. But I insisted. They could choose who to do the job evaluations. We appointed Hays, who had vast experience in job evaluation consultancy. The survey came up with a very interesting finding. It uncovered that there were people who had come from GEC Marconi after the 1999 merger who had stronger attributes than some individuals already on the board, all of whom came from British Aerospace. Part of the cultural issue in the company was that after the merger the executive was dominated by the British Aerospace club.

That report allowed the board to act. I was trying to reduce the number of executive directors on the board. I was also seeking to ensure that these should be the very best the company had to offer and the right people for succession. As a result two of the directors left and Ian King who came from Marconi became the Chief Operating Officer in 2007 and was elevated to the board.

I wanted to ensure there should be regular reviews of the board effectiveness of each member, in accordance with the Combined Code. I required external facilitators to conduct the board effectiveness reviews. I wanted a man and a woman to maximise the range of interpersonal skills. I felt they would say more to a woman than they would to a man. Anyway, it was brilliant. It was absolutely brilliant. We had Ashley Sommerfield from Egon Zehnder and an independent and experienced board performance consultant, Sheena Crane. Each time we had an effectiveness review, I had a one-on-one conversation with every board member. Of course the senior independent director hauled me in for a one-on-one conversation about my performance.

The board effectiveness process had a couple of added benefits. It gave me information and insight about the strengths and weaknesses of the individual non-executive directors. Each board member also gave their view of the effectiveness of their colleagues in one-on-one sessions.

That led to changes on the board. Lord Hesketh left and we gave him a farewell dinner. From then on, I instituted a practice whereby we had a dinner for any retiring member of the board. I would ask other members of the board who had served in that person's time to join us for dinner. We did that throughout my ten years at BAE.

A slightly more troubling question arose over Michael Portillo, the former defence secretary. Michael Portillo had not been on the board for that long: he joined in September 2002. The issue with him was that he also wrote articles for newspapers. In an article in *The Sunday Times* on 19 June 2005, he questioned the government's policy on maintaining a nuclear deterrent. But building nuclear-powered submarines and submarines armed with nuclear warheads was not only a very key part of the government's defence strategy. It was a very key part of the company's business. We had over a thousand apprenticeships for young people in Barrow-in-Furness where the submarines were built. I am quite sure many of these young people might otherwise have posed a problem to society. They ended up being really strong members of society because they were trained by the company in electrical engineering, electronics, welding and many other skills.

There were two directions that he could go. One was that he stopped writing articles in the newspapers in the area of defence and he stayed on the board. Alternatively he could leave the board and continue to write whatever he wanted in the newspapers and pursue all his other media interests. He decided he would stick with his media interests.[8] So I said, fine. We would have a party. We should always act with civility.

I wanted Americans to be represented on the board. It was staggering there were no American non-executive directors. Much of the company was in America. Some things were for American eyes only. So I needed the board to have some American competence and capability. It was Peter Sutherland, chairman of Goldman Sachs International as well as chairman of BP, who came up with the suggestion for my first appointment. Peter Weinberg at the time was running Goldman Sachs outside the US, based in London. Peter Sutherland told him he really needed to go and help me; that I had got all sorts of issues. On 16 June 2005 Peter Weinberg was appointed to the board.

In September 2005, Roberto Quarta, an Italian-born American and British businessman, a partner in the private equity firm Clayton, Dubilier & Rice and a world expert in mergers and acquisitions, joined the board.

He was an excellent director, thanks to his huge experience in industrial businesses. He had been found by Julia Budd, of Zygos executive search consultants who dealt with board appointments. We had appointed them to search for candidates.

I asked Phil Carroll to join too. He was President and Chairman of Fluor Corporation, an oil services contractor, and previously had been the head of Shell in the US. He was a high quality, super person. Julia Budd had spoken to him. Phil wanted to know more. He came to London often. I went to see Phil at his club. He said he had discussed the proposal with his lawyer who told him that he had got to this stage in life. He had done extremely well. Why would he want to take on the risk of being an independent director for a defence company in the United Kingdom? Furthermore they would pay him nothing.

I told him, it was indeed less than £100,000 a year – not much for an American – depending on what committees he sat on. However it was fascinating work. Somebody once told me I had the most interesting job in London. It combined money, technology, government and politics. Where else did those things come so close together?

Within a few months we had gone from having no American non-executive directors on the board to having three. It was very useful to have their US perspective and experience, particularly given the increasing importance of BAE's operations in the US which was to reach 50% of sales. We were also expanding: we acquired United Defense in mid-2005, making the BAE the second largest land systems company in the world.

We were doing other things to improve governance. The Board agreed a Board Charter covering a number of principles of governance. These included strategy, standards and values, and oversight and controls. It also laid out clearly the principal duties of the chairman and the chief executive. It was important to have these issues written down and enacted.

CHAPTER 21

# Change Agent

It was about this time that Alastair Imrie head of HR came to me with what he called a very minor issue. The general counsel was over 60. According to our policies the chairman had to sign each year for the general counsel to continue in his job. One could ask why this decision had to be taken by the chairman and not by the chief executive. The general counsel at BAE Michael Lester had been the personal lawyer to Lord Weinstock, chairman of GEC. At BAE he also sat on the board as legal director. When Alastair approached me about extending Michael Lester's contract beyond the normal retirement age, I told him I was really very happy to sign it this time but I would never sign it again.

What that did was to create another piece of change. For the executive then had to go off and search for a new general counsel. Some months later the executive came back to me. They asked if I would like to meet the person they thought was going to be the next general counsel. I said I would love to. And so one Philip Bramwell came into my office. It was the first time I had ever met him. He was general counsel of O2. We had a one hour and a half conversation and I thought he was absolutely great. I did not share my thoughts with anybody. I could see that this was a really good change. Because Philip Bramwell was a change agent. I was not sure the executive realised he was a change agent. I told the executive he was a wonderful choice and they should go ahead.

I learnt later that while considering the job Philip had sought the counsel of the grand old man of the city, the former chairman of Cazenove, David Mayhew. He intimated the company was up a very dirty creek without a paddle. The admiral on the bridge (i.e. me!) was the only way of getting it sorted. Never was there greater need. The general counsel had been in

## 21. CHANGE AGENT

charge of our response to the SFO, sending van loads of documents to them. Philip joined BAE at the end of 2006. Unlike Michael Lester he did not have a seat on the board; but he always sat in on board meetings.

He was the first senior executive the company had ever recruited from outside. There were reasons why BAE promoted from within. In some areas, such as the building of nuclear-powered submarines, there were requirements of strict confidentiality. And the boats are so complex the skills needed to build them are acquired over a life-time. BAE Systems still had Other Government Departments status. This means that in certain circumstances, like the granting of security clearances, it operates as a government entity. It has powers devolved to it of government. BAE controlled, and still controls, Portsmouth Naval Dockyard. Most people in the business knew no other. They joined at 18 and left on retirement. However the bigger reason why BAE operated as a sealed unit was that it operated like a relay team: the baton was handed to someone else on the team, not from outside. This was something that with the arrival of Philip was going to change.

He was the right person at the right time. His arrival really brought inside the company the first person in the executive I felt was likeminded. He shared my conviction we should move from back foot to front foot. This was invaluable for me personally. He was the man I could – and did – turn to in time of need. He arrived not a moment too soon.

The executive began to take a wider view of the world. And the company began engaging more with NGOs. One of my early experiences at BAE was of an NGO wanting to come and speak to the company. I had come from a background where it is much better to communicate with, engage with, and discuss with NGOs. Otherwise things could get out of hand.

I was not able to spend much time with Philip at that time. For I was going to be out of the office. Getting away from it all.

CHAPTER 22

# Atlantic Rally

For years I had been itching to sail the Atlantic. Claire, as a doctor, gently suggested for me it was now or never: I was not getting any younger. The opportunity provided was to take part in the Atlantic Rally for Cruisers. This was very different from the Round the World race challenge with *BP Explorer*. This was on my Discovery 55, *More Magic,* with only four crew, including myself. As the name suggested it was not a race, but a rally. Although we all treated it as a race.

We were to set off from Las Palmas in the Gran Canarias on 26 November 2006, bound for St Lucia 3,000 sea miles away. I had rearranged the dates of the board meetings to allow me maximum time to prepare and take part in the ARC. We shifted the last one of the year to 15 November in Rosslyn. The first one of 2007 was pushed back to the end of January. This gave me six weeks.

I had two friends who were keen and experienced sailors. One was a gynaecological surgeon. He might have been eminent in his field but we had to send him off to do a resuscitation refresher course. The other was a toxicologist. Like me he went off and did diesel engineering courses and other basic maintenance.

Tony Bottrell, who was the watch leader on *BP Explorer,* was our fourth person. I realised that we were all in our sixties or thereabouts and we needed someone younger on board. Then just weeks before we were due to start Tony said he could not make it for family reasons. I turned to Chay Blyth to bail me out. I told him I needed a young person in case someone needed to clamber up the mast. He gave me two CVs: one of a young lady and one of a young man. We chose the young lady. Hannah Jenner said she had nothing much on at the time and I asked her to join us. She was amazing. If something went wrong, she was the first person under the floor with a spanner. And of course things did go wrong. We had two huge foresails, with two big poles to keep them set. When the wind got really high, we had to roll them in. The furlers that were meant to roll in the sails failed. There was a 30 knot wind behind us. I can picture Hannah sitting on the push pit right on the bow of the boat, with a handful of tools, trying to rethread the rope round a drum, which was the furling device, of the genoa, the bigger of the two foresails which we had. When you are in the middle of an ocean, there is no alternative but to fix every problem yourself.

We had all sorts of other issues. There was a moment when all the instruments were telling me that we were losing power. In a boat like that, with few crew, much of the work was done with power-assisted machines or gadgets. We were soaking up huge amounts of power with the self-steering gear, the freezers and fridges and watermakers. We were running the generator eight hours a day to charge it up. Hannah was unperturbed. The lights looked all right, she said. What was the problem? She was right. In the end, I exchanged emails with Vetco and the people who made all the electronics. I decided just to recalibrate the whole thing. We did not have another problem. But it kept me awake for day after day because I thought we were going to be dark in three days. Four people are really not enough to sail a boat like that unassisted. We needed self-steering. And we needed electricity.

Hannah became the skipper of *Glasgow* afterwards. She was the skipper when they lost somebody overboard, 800 miles from South Africa. Somehow they got them back in the middle of the night.

The girls had done a fantastic job of planning and preparing every meal for 20 days. We had a freezer. I can remember doing fillet steaks 1000 miles from land in the evening. And we smoked huge cigars – though I have never smoked cigarettes. We made bread every day. We had a water maker, so we had showers every day. It was completely different from the spartan Around the World yacht.

We caught the trade winds south-west of the Canary Islands, just north of the Cape Verde islands. With 30 knots of wind behind us rolling was pretty amazing. The trade winds were very, very good for the crossing. It was exhilarating. The 55-foot Discovery was a really good boat, so I was never worried about safety. We had sat-phones and I could do email too.

BUILDING BRIDGES

I kept in touch with the office and spoke with Mike Turner using an Iridium sat phone from the middle of the Atlantic. We were filling in logs. We were obviously checking a lot of things on the boat. When you are racing, you cannot do anything else. You have to concentrate on sailing the entire time. This was more relaxed – but we made excellent time.

We made the crossing in a little over 15 days, averaging over eight knots. We came fifth in a class of 22 boats. I was very pleased to see that we arrived before the other 55 owned by a friend of mine. We also got there before Philip Hampton, Chairman of GSK, who was in the same class, in his Oyster 49 which was smaller than ours.

CHAPTER 23

# TNK-BP

At about the same time I was trying to disengage from TNK-BP. The Russia story for BP started with the collapse of the Berlin wall. Until then, the Soviet Union had been off limits to foreign oil companies. But we had to have dealings with Russia. I always said to people, if you want to understand the oil industry, you need to remain friends with Saudi Arabia, because they have the oil; and you need to remain friends in Russia because of the gas. Russia for us was the greatest prize on earth. It had immense natural resources, in minerals, oil and gas. Russia has more gas reserves than anywhere else. It was a hugely attractive prospect. It also has large oil reserves: it is in the top three producers in the world. However output was declining because of a lack of new technology and some outdated practices. They did a lot of drilling rigidly on grids rather than choosing more precisely where they should be drilling.

Within five months of the wall coming down we were in Russia scouting the territory and in 1990 BP opened an office in Moscow. We knew something was happening and we had to be part of it.

Perestroika brought the opening up of Russia to a more liberal economic regime. This - initially - resulted in the destruction of a huge amount of GDP. That then forced the young people who were all deputy prime ministers, like Boris Nemtsov and Anatoly Chubais, into raising money by selling off state assets.

I knew Nemtsov - who was shot dead on a bridge in 2015 after opposing Putin's annexation of Crimea - and Chubais who I thought was very sensible. John and I went to see Chubais at the Russian Embassy in Kensington Palace Gardens. There were the three of us and an interpreter. Chubais started the meeting with a very long Russian introduction, all of which was then repeated in English by the interpreter. When he had finished, John started, and John did not pause for the interpreter. So I said, perhaps a little pause. Chubais looked at me and said in perfect English, "He started so he might as well carry on". And the rest of the meeting went on in perfect English – without the interpreter.

The most successful acquirer of the oil shares, and one of the wealthiest men in Russia today, was Vladimir Potanin. He was the first Russian oligarch I knew. During the Soviet regime, he had worked in the state foreign trade organisation. In the post-Soviet years, he founded a bank and became a keen proponent of economic reform. He was a supporter of Chubais. Potanin personally benefitted hugely from the privatisation of state industries especially in oil, gas and minerals: his bank acquired Sidanco, one of the largest oil companies in Russia. It owned Kovytka, a massive gas field near Irkutsk.

The deal to sell Sidanco in this state auction had been made possible by loans provided by a Brit and an American. Joe Lewis was very wealthy in those days. He had made a fortune in currency exchange. But £3bn today does not get you into the top rank of the super-wealthy. He lived close to Michael Dingman, the ranking director of the Ford Motor Company, in the exclusive gated community of Lyford Cay in the Bahamas.

In effect, Joe Lewis and Michael Dingman lent money to Vladimir Potanin. Potanin in turn lent the money to the Russian government. In return they received the shares of OAO Sidanco. The Russian government never repaid the loans to take the shares back. As far as I know, in none of these deals did that happen. The government was made up of individuals. Individuals have mixed motives, including personal motives. What is likely to have happened is that when companies like Sibneft were sold, money went into the hands of individuals.

Sidanco was an integrated oil company. They did upstream and downstream. They owned the drilling companies, the service companies, and the transport companies. It was also much more than that. It and other companies like it owned everything. They owned the people – it had 100,000 employees. They owned the towns where the workers worked. They owned the medical centre, the schools, the flats, the holiday homes: everything.

In late 1997 BP acquired a 10% stake in Sidanco. We paid six times more than Bill Browder's Hermitage Fund had done a couple of years before, but it was still to prove a brilliant and massively rewarding first step into

Russia. Jack Golden and I became directors of Sidanco – even though Jack was not keen to go to Russia.

In the early days, when we were doing Sidanco with Vladimir Potanin, we would go and talk to the government. The meeting would be planned with Boris Nemtsov. I was instructed to get in a car and go through the front door. Potanin would get into his car, blue lights on the roof, zoom down to the Kremlin and by the time I got into the room, he would already be there sitting on the same side of the table and next to Boris Nemtsov. Without making any sweeping generalisation about the power and influence of oligarchs as a group, I observed at first hand that the connection between Vladimir Potanin and the Russian government was incredibly close. After all they were mutually beneficial.

Potanin was in my office in London the day before the famous meeting with Putin, which has been aired in television documentaries. We were chatting, and he said he had got to go back to Moscow that night. I asked him why. They had a meeting with Putin the next day, he replied. I asked him what Putin was going to say. He said Putin was going to tell them that they could keep their gains so long as they did not meddle in politics. And of course, that is exactly what happened the following day.

However within a couple of years, we were to experience a major setback. We had a period where actually Sidanco became bankrupt. It was the only company I have ever been a director of that became bankrupt, which caused me terrible problems. For when you are seeking nomination as a company director, you have to declare if you have ever been a director of a bankrupt company. I had to say, yes: OAO Sidanco. This went on for about 15 years. It became an issue for me.

In November 1999 we had suddenly found that Sidanco's prize Chernogorneft oil and gas unit had been sold for a song at a bankruptcy auction to the Tyumen Oil Company (Tyumenskaya Neftyanaya Kompaniya, hence TNK) controlled by another oligarch, Mikhail Fridman. At a stroke our investment in Sidanco plummeted in value.

We had a choice. We could either cut our losses and get out. Or we could stand and fight.

We decided to stand and fight. We sued TNK in the Russian courts. This was a risky strategy. We had little confidence that the courts would find favour with a western company over Russian interests. We also moved globally. We used the company's influence in the US and the State

Department blocked a half billion dollar loan that TNK was seeking from the Exim bank. By this time of course the merger with Amoco had taken place. BP was now a bigger company than it had been in 1997. And it was the largest producer of oil and gas in the United States. It was also the largest owner of reserves in the US. It was a player in Washington.

The British prime minister was also supporting us as part of his policy of trying to encourage investment in Russia. This he hoped would draw Russia into a more pro-western orbit. In March 2000 Tony Blair had flown to St Petersburg two weeks before the Russian presidential election, to show his support for the candidature of the city's mayor Vladimir Putin. The next month, president-elect Putin made his first official visit to London. There, before going to Downing Street, Putin addressed business leaders at a Confederation of British Industry seminar in Whitehall. I was one of them. It was the only time I met him. We were all told that we could ask one question. I said it was clear that Russia needed foreign direct investment. In order to do so we required the judiciary and the legal system to work properly. He of course knew how a court had deprived us of Chernogorneft. He said, "Yes, Mr. Olver, you're quite right. You'll understand that the judiciary could be open to corruption, because we haven't paid them for five years". I walked away and thought, the good news about that was he understood the problem.

Some questioned our strategy of persisting. There was one meeting at BP's headquarters. We had experts on everything there: subsurface experts, geophysicists, geologists, seismologists, reservoir and production engineers, the whole nine yards. We went through everything with Joe Lewis. The meeting went on for some time. At some point, I turned to Joe on my left, and I said, that while we had got everybody here, he could ask any question he liked. What could we help him with in understanding where this company was? And Joe turned to me and said that it was very sweet of me but he would just like to know why we were doing this. So I told it was very simple. We did not like to lose. He was intimating that it was all a bit of a problem and that we should move on and do something else. Whereas the BP way was to fix any problem that we faced. Certainly, my view was that we would leave no stone unturned in making sure that this worked out well.

And it did. At least until Russia invaded Ukraine twenty years later.

In 2002 we decided to double down on BP's stake in Sidanco. BP acquired a further 15% of the company, raising its stake to 25%.

## 23. TNK-BP

We had a very interesting period. I think John had already decided that the only real issue was to do a deal with Mikhail Fridman and TNK. If you cannot beat them, join them. But he was going to test the water elsewhere first. Whether it was to amuse me or what I do not know, but he suggested I go and talk to the chief executives of all the companies and come back and tell him who I thought we should do business with. We were looking at all the companies which might have been a fit for us, and of course much depended on the individuals who controlled them.

That is when I met Mikhail Khodorkovsky, who owned Yukos, then the largest oil company in Russia. He was one of the wealthiest people, if not the wealthiest person, at that time. We met at the Savoy. He was extremely polished. He knew exactly what he was doing. He had a very switched-on chief financial officer who was an American. It was a very interesting meeting. He was very, very slick. And I worried about quite how we might get on with him.

My most interesting encounter was with a man called Vladimir Bogdanov. Bogdanov was the Chief Executive Officer of Surgutneftegaz, another massive oil company. He was an engineer. He never met anybody who was not Russian. Not for nothing was he known as the Hermit of Siberia. He rarely came to Moscow and he made no attempt to court western oil companies. Until me. So it was amazing that I actually had a meeting with him.

Our first meeting was in Moscow. He told me to come and see him in his office. I asked him where that was. Surgut, Siberia, I was told. We flew to Moscow, refuelled, and then flew east. There was absolutely nothing to see. It was pitch black. It felt like three hours in the air. After we landed we went into a town of high-rise apartment buildings, with little balconies that had been covered in with glass or plastic. It was bitterly cold. One building stood out above all the others, such as you might have seen in New York. This was the hotel and the office of Surgutneftegaz, the fourth largest oil company in Russia. That is where we stayed. Our hotel rooms were superb: it was like being in the Four Seasons in New York. The following day we went to the office. It was much the finest office I had ever been into anywhere in the world. You entered through enormous floor-to-ceiling curved doors.

Why did he see us? Somehow we must have indicated to him that we were interested. The interaction was on a very human level. It was engineer to engineer. I did not come with a load of hubris. Maybe he found it a bit strange. He could see the appeal of doing something with us. It emerged soon enough that we each had different wishes. After a long conversation and exchange of emails afterwards, it was clear he was looking for some sort of supply deal. I actually thought that this would be a more serious arrangement and that we could be equal partners with him. We were looking for a partner for a mega merger to create a huge and wonderful modern company that would be one of the biggest companies not only in Russia but across the world. He just could not get his head around that. I think he lacked imagination. I do not think he was frightened. He probably did not want to give up being the king of the castle. Nor did he want to be joint king of the castle.

We ended up creating TNK-BP. The two adversaries, after four years of often acrimonious tussle, decided to join forces. The acrimony would frequently reappear. But for years the two sides had a mutually successful relationship. We contributed Sidanco and they contributed TNK. We added BP's assets in Russia, in the downstream: a string of petrol stations and other things. We also paid about $7 billion – the biggest foreign investment ever in Russia at that time. TNK-BP was a huge company which ended up producing 2 million barrels a day. The split was 50-50, which was highly unusual in Russia, if not actually unique. The one stipulation was that the chairman had to be Russian: Mikhail Fridman. His Alfa Bank owned 25% of the stock; Len Blavatnik and Viktor Vekselberg were other directors, each with 12.5%. German Khan was an executive director, and they co-opted a tall Frenchman who had been chief executive of Elf that became Total. Another person who was to serve on the supervisory board of TNK-BP was the former German Chancellor Gerhard Schröder.

In the context of Russia, Len was very important because he was an American citizen. He was therefore subject to the Foreign Corrupt Practices Act. He grew up in the Ukraine, in Odessa, and then moved to the States and was educated at Harvard. As a result on the other side of the table, I had somebody who really understood the Western world, the language and culture of the West, and understood what we needed to see in terms of behaviour and ethics. So if there was a major issue, Len could often figure out how to help solve the problem. And we did have problems.

The agreement was signed in London in front of Prime Minister Tony

Blair and President Putin, who was in Britain on a state visit: Putin had tea with the Queen. The signing took place on the margins of an international oil conference at Lancaster House. It was entitled "Russia-UK: Long term partnership". That was the feeling at the time. Putin described Britain as one of Russia's most significant European partners. Blair told the conference that "the things that bind us together in politics, security and economics are very important. Together we can achieve our mutual goals of global stability, economic growth and international development." How the world has changed.

In Putin's first term, which is now a long way away, government employees had not been paid. It was a complete disaster. Things improved but we still had legal issues. Simple issues like an individual executive not getting their work permit renewed. Normally you would use your partners to deal with such issues. So long as they wanted the same outcome. But we also helped develop the work force so that they increasingly took decisions themselves and gained greater work satisfaction as a result. We revolutionised the safety performance in TNK-BP. Safety became a greater priority.

Having been on the board at BP and Reuters, I was not used to board meetings ending in a row when half the board stood up and walked out. I certainly had not seen it elsewhere because they did not have that problem elsewhere. But we did have that situation with TNK-BP. In the end, I told Mikhail we were going to meet the night before board meetings. He asked why. I said we were going to sort out what problems were going to come up the next day and figure out what to do about them beforehand. He accepted that. And that was what we did.

My initiative worked. It was not simple to manage. It was very difficult and hard work for our 200 expatriates in the company. And particularly, of course, for the Chief Executive Officer who at the time was Bob Dudley. Nobody could have done a better job in extraordinarily difficult conditions. He should get a medal for his work in Russia.

The Russians wanted to get to know us. Mikhail was saying we needed to go off-site and learn about each other. He used the word 'bond'. In the end, I succumbed. A time was arranged for us to go to Alpha bank's facility a fair way north of Moscow. It was not a quick car journey. Mikhail very kindly offered the use of his helicopter. I said I would happily accept a ride in his helicopter. We went on the helicopter together. There were always risks travelling in Russia. History will show that the chief executive of Sidanco some years before had died on his executive jet. It was not an unknown event.

When we got there, it was a bit like Amoco's Red Crown Lodge in Wisconsin. Different buildings were set in a beautiful landscape. There was a central hall and we ate incredibly well. Most striking was going to an area that had hot and cold baths. A man would beat us with a large birch stick. Then I was running across the grass and jumping into the Volga River with Mikhail Fridman, stark naked. It was cold! So when people since have asked how well I knew Mikhail Fridman I have been able to reply truthfully, really quite well.

Did seeing someone without any clothes on who I faced across a table make any difference to doing business? It probably did, tactically. In terms of day-to-day life and board meetings. But strategically it did not make any difference. When you have done something very different, something off-site, and then sat around a table drinking tea, it might help to understand each other. I do not think it made him or me a softer touch when it came to making a decision.

We had an exclusivity agreement. However it was confined to Russia. At one stage, the TNK directors wanted to buy a refinery in Lithuania. They probably said it was in the Russian part of Lithuania. We could have had the Ukraine situation all over again. It was one of those occasions that half the board got up and left the meeting. We never bought the refinery.

I served as deputy chairman for two years and three months. But during that period we were hunting for somebody who could ultimately take over from me. We found Lord Robertson, who as a former defence secretary and secretary general of Nato had his own deep knowledge of Russia. I knew George quite well. I had had lots of conversations with him about what to expect in Russia. There was never an issue about my being chairman of a defence company and also deputy chairman of a company that was Russian. As far as I am aware, no one on the British side suggested there was an incompatibility or a possible security risk.

By the time I had left, I think we had dividended back the $7 billion it cost. So it was nil net cost, but it was a million barrels a day per day of production for each of TNK and BP, something like half the company's reserves. It was huge, which of course became the issue later.

CHAPTER 24

# Back to BAE Systems: Salvaging Reputation

THE ROCKET THAT was the SFO enquiry completely side-tracked me from what I was trying to achieve. The priority now was reputation. The reputation of the company. And by extension, the reputation of those who worked for the company, including myself. It was a time of crisis. Any time of crisis is a test for every individual. When the reputation of the enterprise is being questioned, that is a time when a chairman ceases to be non-executive. You have to change gear. That is why I was leading. It was me that suggested that we had a review. It showed what should be done.

The reputation of BAE, if the press was a guide, was embarrassing. Even before I joined, it was named in investigations into alleged corruption in its Saudi business. The company's image and reputation were seriously tarnished in public opinion. I had to act decisively.

The board under my chairmanship was not a board that got lost in governance and process. It was accountable for monitoring performance. There was a lot of performance at the board. We were involved in real things. Such as, who should be running this company? Why was the performance so all over the place? From 25% in Saudi Arabia to next to nothing in the UK. How were we to get performance to be a 10% return on sales everywhere? Improving performance was what we were all there for. I had come from a company where performance and benchmarking were instilled in one from the outset. The strategic review I had initiated as soon as I joined BAE was to examine where the future of the company lay. On a tactical level, I wanted to ensure that the way we made our products was the best for the company and for our customers. It was essential that there was alignment of views with the executive.

Disputes over the contracts for building aircraft carriers that had been publicly aired before my arrival were to rumble on after I became chairman. The company had said they could not have a fixed price contract because the Navy and MoD kept on changing their minds on the design of the carriers they were commissioning. These changes of mind were not minor details. They were fundamental to how the carrier-borne aircraft were to be launched. First, the MoD wanted a ramp. This was the design innovation first introduced by the Royal Navy during WWII. It gave uplift to the aircraft so they could be launched at lower speeds from shorter runways – and therefore could be accommodated by smaller ships. Then they said they wanted to use a catapult, the system used by most larger US aircraft carriers and on most others in service around the world. However the Royal Navy/MoD were asking not for the more common steam catapult used by the US Navy but an electro-magnetic catapult – a largely untested technology.

This was not a way to run a commercial contract. I had come from an industry where we worked with the operators how to build an offshore platform. Once we decided what we were going to do, we froze it. Nobody made any changes. The costs were fixed.

The MoD had proposed a different kind of contractual arrangement: an alliance. The French company Thales, Babcock and BAE would build the carriers. This was not an arrangement that BAE Systems executive had sanctioned before. They had always favoured a contractual form that had them as the lead contractor with everybody else subcontracted to them. That was their model. They had no experience of an alliance.

My experience with the Andrew Field at BP had made me a keen advocate of the alliance approach. For the aircraft carriers, we would have a target price. The alliance partners would share the risk and reward, above and below – as we had found at BP. If our costs rose, we would start to lose margin. If our costs were below projected, we would gain. The whole idea with an alliance was that each member shared in everybody's success. It was in the interests of each and every party to help a partner that was struggling. The common aim was to deliver on time and below budget.

However, I had to be convinced that the alliance on the carriers was working. So for example I opposed the wish of the alliance building the carriers to appointing KBR to manage their construction. KBR's project management expertise lay mainly in the oil and gas sector, as I knew well.

## 24. BACK TO BAE SYSTEMS

We felt they lacked the requisite skills to manage such a complex project as building aircraft carriers.

As an engineer I was also flummoxed by the way that ships were built. I knew something about the construction of other massive floating marine structures. Oil platforms are built by in effect bolting modular sections with all their contents directly on top of the jacket, the skeleton of the platform. Submarines are also built in a more modular way. You actually fill a section of the tube with all that it needs and then put these tubes together.

When we were building ships, the method was to build the hull and then start doing the insides. No one wanted to change, or even to explore the possibility of a different approach. When I suggested building ships in a modular way, so you could simply slot in parts where required, I was told, we cannot do that. They insisted that they could not have joints in cables. So they would run miles of miles of cables through ships, from bow to stern and stern to bow. Other industries manage to bolt sections together, with connections for cables, but not naval shipbuilding.

In 2006, we made what appeared to be a major strategic decision. In reality it had less consequence than some had predicted. The executive proposed that we sell our 20% stake in Airbus. On the face of it that would mean getting out of civil aviation.

The executive's proposal was discussed by the board. The board agreed to what was being proposed. There were no real synergies between the civil and defence side. A 20% stake was not large enough to give us any control over decisions. It was a sort of passive investment. The argument was that the industry was cyclical, that in a downturn in the defence business the civil aviation side could compensate. At 20% it was not big enough to make such a material difference. That is the reason why the board agreed to the executive's proposal.

By the end of 2006, pressure was growing on the government to halt the SFO enquiry. Britain's ambassador to Saudi Arabia Sir Sherard Cowper-Coles had warned the SFO and the Solicitor General of threats senior Saudis had made. They warned that unless the SFO ended the investigation, Britain risked grave damage to economic relations and an end to cooperation in confronting extremism. Two days after the ambassador spoke to the Solicitor General, the SFO announced the end of the enquiry into Al-Yamamah.

Tony Blair explained the decision by saying Britain did not want to upset our Saudi friends. We could not afford to have a security spat with Saudi Arabia. We would risk people being killed in the streets. His words were unfortunate. Fear of upsetting the Saudis was not the reason in my view why the SFO had to end the enquiry. The real reason was that everything BAE did was in accordance with the contract. Tony Blair was never going to admit that in fact his government and previous governments had made this deal. They had signed the document! They were party to the contract and its terms. That is why I said to Gus O'Donnell, the cabinet secretary, right at the beginning, that I would lie down for Britain but he had to help.

Based on everything I had seen and the discussions I had with real experts, there was no case to answer. This view was echoed by the judge who reviewed the SFO decision to end its investigation. Lord Justice Moses (Sir Alan Moses) lambasted the SFO for giving into pressure from the government to close the enquiry. But he said that BAE had not done anything wrong: "BAE has always contended that any payments it made were approved by the Kingdom of Saudi Arabia. In short they were lawful commissions and not secret payments made without the consent or approval of the principal ... It would be unfair to BAE to assume that there was a realistic possibility, let alone a probability, of proving that it was guilty of any criminal offence."

Even after changing the board I still faced a torrent of newspaper articles about BAE and its dealings with the Saudis. Everything from Rolls-Royces round the back of Harrods to women provided for individuals. It just would not stop. I really did think we needed to have an independent review of the ethical performance of the company. This was nothing to do with what was being looked at by the Serious Fraud Office. We needed to do this for the sake of our company. My objective was to review the state of the ethical performance of the company from bottom to top and to make recommendations if necessary about what needed to be changed. I had rebalanced the board by shrinking executive numbers and increasing the number of non-executives. I had a board that would back me.

Who would or could conduct this review? I had a number of people in mind. The first person I contacted was Lord Robertson. I had lunch with George and told him what I was thinking of doing. He said that was a really good idea. But clearly he could not do it because he had signed off

## 24. BACK TO BAE SYSTEMS

on the Al-Yamamah business when he was defence secretary. We had a very agreeable lunch and I walked back into my office and asked Janet to call the eminent Lord Woolf. He had been Master of the Rolls and had recently retired as Lord Chief Justice of England and Wales: these were the top judicial posts in England. He was also held in very high esteem by his legal colleagues as one of the great judicial reformers. I told Janet to ask him if he would like breakfast with me. She told me I did not know Lord Woolf. She was right. I did not. But I would still love to have breakfast with him. Would she call him?

She called Lord Woolf at his office. He said I should come to his club. I sat with him by the window in the Athenaeum. We had a very nice breakfast and I explained to him what I wanted to do. He said – he addressed me as "My dear boy", which made me feel better already – that he did not think he had got one of the attributes that we needed and that we were looking for. I told him – I called him Lord Woolf: I didn't call him Harry till later – he had the only attribute that I needed. Unimpeachable integrity. He was taken aback by this. But he said he ought to do some due diligence. Again, I had the wrong end of the stick. Because I asked him how I could help him with that. Would he like some introductions close to the firm? Did he want to talk to the auditors? No, he retorted. He was going to do due diligence on *me*.

Shortly afterwards, in April, I was staying at Ca's Xorc hotel on the mountainous north coast of Mallorca. It was a beautiful old building and I had invited 30 or 40 people to dinner to celebrate Pam's sixtieth birthday. The phone went. It was Harry Woolf. He said he had done his due diligence on me and he would do the job. Indeed, as he was to recount in his memoir,[9] he did check up on my reputation and sounded out the government as to whether they were in favour of his undertaking this commission, which he was assured they were.

He also stated that more important to him than the company's cooperation was the impression he formed "as to Dick Olver's integrity and competence. Here my views were entirely favourable. I would have been astonished if he let me down."

I was delighted. Again I asked if there was anything I could do to help him. He said he would need some other people. I told him I would arrange that and get anybody he required. He said he wanted somebody who worked with a big firm, somebody who understood finance, and somebody with a pen. I told him to leave that with me for a couple of weeks and I would sort it all out for him.

I called the managing director of the Institute of Business Ethics, Philippa Foster Back. I told her I wanted her – and that I needed somebody with a pen who understood business ethics. She said there was an independent committee sponsored by the cabinet office: the Committee on Standards in Public Life. Its secretary Dr Richard Jarvis understood all questions of ethics and business ethics. The committee was not doing much at that time. I spoke to the cabinet secretary Gus O'Donnell about him and told him I needed him. I told Gus it was in his interests that the project got done well. He told me to leave it with him. He called me back a week later and told me I could have him. So I got Richard Jarvis.

I called my old friend from the Reuters board, Sir David Walker, who was writing the report on private equity. I told him we needed his help. I had to have somebody who understood business and finance to help Lord Woolf on his ethics committee for BAE. He said he was sorry but he was completely snowed under. He had to finish the report. I told David I needed his help. David agreed. What a wonderful man.

Then I spoke to Doug Daft, an Australian who had been the Chief Executive Officer of Coca-Cola: he fitted Lord Woolf's requirement for someone who worked for a big firm. He too agreed.

The board formally appointed Lord Woolf on 15 June 2007. His committee was tasked with reporting on BAE's ethical policies and processes and reviewing the company's adherence to anti-corruption legislation, including international treaty obligations. It was also asked to measure BAE's policies and procedures against industry standards, and to assess whether they were robust enough to detect and prevent violations of anti-corruption laws. Finally, the committee was to recommend any remedial actions it felt that the BAE Group should take.

I met Harry and we walked in the park. He asked me what I really wanted. I told him I wanted a world class company. I did not want just what was good. I wanted it to be the best in the world. Harry was great. He said that was absolutely where he was. What we had to do was to describe for BAE, but also for others, what was required to be a world class multinational company working in the twenty-first century. That was what we were going to do.

Lord Woolf was aware that the company was the subject of a considerable

## 24. BACK TO BAE SYSTEMS

amount of adverse publicity and criticism. He knew that "the company had strenuously denied it had done anything wrong. It denied making any unlawful payments over the Al-Yamamah contracts. However it was also prevented in its view from giving its account of what it did for reasons of national security."[10]

I got Lord Woolf all these people and an office away from everywhere else. I told him I had started a corporate responsibility committee and that he should meet the members. He could have access to all of them and to any members of the board and anywhere in the company that he wanted. This he did – in an ingenious way. Harry was wonderful. One could write a book on his contribution. One of the things he did was to go round the world meeting people who had the same birthday as he did. That gave him a diagonal slice of the 100,000-employee company. So he would have an apprentice and a mid-ranking person and a senior person and a coffee lady, all in completely different roles and at different levels but with one thing in common: their date of birth.

The appointment of Lord Woolf to head his commission came not a moment too soon. The next month we were notified that the US Department of Justice was launching an investigation into possible corruption over the Al-Yamamah deal. We were now fighting legal battles on both sides of the Atlantic. For the SFO was also investigating other accusations of BAE wrongdoing in South Africa, Tanzania and the Czech Republic.

We were blessed in having Philip Bramwell in charge of our legal strategy. We convened a meeting in the cabinet offices with Gus O'Donnell. The senior adviser to the government was the formidable Daniel Bethlehem QC, the principal legal adviser to the foreign office and an expert of public international law. We needed settlement of the SFO and the DoJ challenges.

The SFO inquiry had not helped our relations with the Saudis. However one bright spot came from an unexpected quarter. In October 2007 I was invited to Buckingham Palace for a state banquet in honour of King Abdullah of Saudi Arabia. When we were introduced in the receiving line the Queen immediately turned to the King and said, "This man is very important to you". Another example of how well briefed she was. I had met the Queen before. On a previous occasion I had been with her at the Grand Military Gold Cup, a horse race for military amateur jockeys at

Sandown Park. I had to name the best dressed horse. Her late Majesty was in the ring and since I had no idea about horses, I asked her for advice. She came alive and told me which one to choose! I watched the race with her and we later gave the prize together.

CHAPTER 25

# Change at the Top

AT THE SAME time, the Mike Turner era was coming to a close. We knew that Mike did not want to retire at 60: he had gone public with the press that he wanted to stay till he was 65. It was in October 2007 that it was announced he would be leaving the following August, when he turned 60. We had had our disagreements. Not over business. More over the way the company did business. Mike and I were open about this. In a joint interview with the FT two years before we said we agreed on strategy; we differed stylistically.[11]

Mike was good at his job. He was bold and tough. He improved the margins of the UK business. But he could be a nightmare in the way he treated people sometimes. He was perceived by some as being frank and forthright, expressing his views to the point of rudeness. We all knew that Mike could be combative: the FT had said officials questioned his leadership, arguing his pugnacious style did the company more harm than good.[12]

The problem was that he seemed vested in the past. The number of times he said to me nothing needed changing. Yet within ten minutes of first walking through the front door, I thought everything needed changing.

Mike was not the only legacy issue I had to address. To my horror, I learned quite early on that Mike Turner had never been to Saudi Arabia. He never had anything to do with Saudi Arabia. The Chief Executive had never been to the country that was the one of the three biggest customers for the company and by far the most profitable one. I asked him why he had not gone. Dick Evans territory, he replied. Dick Evans was the architect of the Saudi Arabian business.

We were left with a very difficult position after Dick left. Dick was the person who had all the relationships with the key princes in Saudi Arabia. He continued to get a consultancy fee after he stepped down.[13]

After he left he started advising the president of Kazakhstan. It was a place I had expressed my opinion of previously. Someone I knew asked my advice about joining a Kazakhstan mining company. I told him that if he was comfortable with knowing that somebody would do something every day in that company not complying with the Foreign Corrupt Practices Act, then he might go ahead. He and his friend joined the board. Then there was a huge bust up and they had to quit.

It was around the same time that I was approached about another job. Andrew Gould the SID at Rio Tinto called me to tell me they needed me. He said I would not have any problem. It was like the oil business: exploration, big capital projects and dealing with governments. I would get my head around it in 10 minutes. Andrew was chief executive of Schlumberger where he had spent almost his entire career so he understood the fit. He was obviously looking for somebody quite urgently. They were in terrible trouble. I thought about it. I was always drawn to places where there were huge problems. I said I would do it, side by side with BAE until my sixth anniversary. This was a time when my chairmanship would in any case be up for review. That would give BAE a couple of years to find a replacement for me. Andrew said that would be great, but they needed someone full time immediately. They wanted someone who would focus on RTZ and nothing else. I could not walk away from BAE and leave it in the lurch. In the end RTZ appointed Jan du Plessis as chairman. RTZ would have been a great job to have done but it just was not to be.

I did another review with Egon Zehnder, this time with David Kidd looking at the position of chief executive. We wondered how wide we could cast the net. I checked with the cabinet office. I argued that so long as the chairman was British, why could not the chief executive be American? The government would not accept it. They insisted that BAE's charter required that both the chairman and chief executive be British citizens. In the end we chose an internal candidate, Ian King, who was then the chief operating officer. He lacked top level international political experience but we would act as a team. Ian would run the company – which he was to do, extremely well. I would continue to help with political relationships around the world.

I had dinner with Ian in Wapping and told him there was one requirement

## 25. CHANGE AT THE TOP

above all other things to being chief executive. When the Woolf report came out it was to be implemented in full. In May 2008, Harry presented his report "Business ethics, global companies and the defence industry. *Ethical business conduct in BAE Systems plc--the way forward*". And to give the engineering company its due, it turned 23 recommendations into more than a thousand action points which were put into effect. Hundreds of discrete changes to the entire policy and process framework of the group. They looked at every conceivable thing. From the quality policy, to expenses, car mileage, gifts and hospitality. Every single policy was reviewed against the principles enshrined in these recommendations. Lawyers drew up the recommendations. Engineers implemented them. Only an engineering company would have the rigour and thinking process to find ways to take a highly complex structure and devise the specific changes to make it comply with new or different design principles. Ian assigned a top project manager from Wharton to oversee the task. We had to get him a new computer as it used so much RAM. In the basement room where he set up his operation there was a massive chart papered over an entire wall. He did what engineers do. He came up with the way forward.

We used those recommendations to embark on the wholesale modernisation of the company. The code of conduct went far beyond the original score or so recommendations. We established twenty-first century standards of responsible business conduct in every aspect of the way the company operated. Its commitment to performance, operational delivery, quality, and workplace culture. Ian really was the right man for that time in the company's history to implement these radical changes. He drummed into his executives quite why the reform was vital. Why it was important. And why it was personal to each and every one of his direct reports, and to each and every one of their direct reports, cascading down through the entire workforce. The effect was to re-engage middle management in what we were doing. This was after a time when they felt distant from the bad press swirling around the company, aimed at the top.

It was a big thing. Not just for us but for UK plc. It did what I hoped: it created the gold standard. I think it still is the gold standard. Some question whether it is possible to be an ethical company in the defence industry. I would argue that being in the defence industry puts a bigger onus on us to make sure that everything we did was to the highest possible standards of business behaviour. We wanted not only to be the most ethical defence contractor; but a company whose business culture was a leader in the corporate world. A top executive of the OECD asked me to lobby the British government to see the legislation adopted in the UK. Indeed our initiative was closely followed by the Law Commission's report proposing reforms to the laws against corruption and bribery and the subsequent UK Bribery Act enacted by parliament.

Many companies read the Woolf report. Some companies instituted bits of it. Unfortunately others did not. Perhaps had some of these companies put in place everything contained in the recommendations, they might have had fewer problems themselves. There were a number of leaders of other companies we were to offer – I think that is the way to put it – to think through their issues because of the incredibly good work that was done here.

To implement the Woolf recommendations to make the group a responsible business worldwide required a massive culture change process. With anywhere between 85,000 and 100,000 people in ten different countries and ten different languages, this was neither quick nor easy. So we developed training modules. We made every single person in the company, from the board down, go through them all. Then we had annual refreshers. We had diagonal slice reviews by external firms. We basically did continuous improvement from the day that Harry gave us the report. Much of it focussed on issues such as conflicts of interest. We were trying to change the culture of the whole massive ecosystem that was BAE. It was an enormous undertaking. But it was necessary and worthwhile.

Of course there were breaches. But we dealt with them. When you were asleep in London you wanted someone in Australia to take the right decision. The only way to ensure that was to have a culture where everybody understood what was the right thing to do. We had incidents that showed not everybody did do the right thing. Did we sometimes, with nearly 85,000 people, have somebody do something silly? Yes. But they did not stay in the company for more than 10 minutes. We had zero tolerance for any misdemeanours or breaches of the company's ethical policies.[14]

All through this period I had been talking to the editors of *The Times*, James Harding, and of the *Financial Times*, Lionel Barber. I was wanting them to realise that things were changing. No stone was left unturned. Once Lord Woolf had been asked to do this review, we committed to ensure that every one of his recommendations, sight unseen, would be

## 25. CHANGE AT THE TOP

put into place. Much excellent work has been done by other people over time in the area of ethics. One such place was Barclays, where David Walker was chairman for a period. Yet I do not know where else anybody actually had the courage to commit up front, not knowing what these recommendations were going to be, to putting them in place. I think that made a huge difference to the press. The *Financial Times* had an article which said, Dick is drawing a line under this. It was a turning point. Everything was now changing.

Even before the Woolf report was commissioned, Philip had started to implement the rules around advisers. He had already embarked on getting rid of agents. He had stopped the group marketing budget. When people came to him to complain that they could no longer access funds he told them he had suspended all payments. He cancelled the contracts of 247 advisers. He had put in place a completely new process, chaired by lawyers external to the company. Executives had to persuade this panel that a particular individual should be proposed to act on behalf of the company. To my knowledge, you could count on the fingers of one hand the number of people that over the next five or ten years actually got through that process. When Lord Woolf reviewed what Philip had done, he declared it a world class vetting process. So when it came to settling with the US Department of Justice we were ahead of the game.

Or so we hoped.

CHAPTER 26

# *Threats and Opportunities Abroad*

T**HE US AUTHORITIES** certainly showed they were deadly serious. There were some uncomfortable moments for some of us. One of the non-executive directors Sir Nigel Rudd was briefly detained when he landed at Houston airport and served with a subpoena by officials from the Department of Justice. The same fate occurred to Mike Turner on arrival in the US. Officials took his BlackBerry and his computer and examined them closely. They questioned him and let him go.

I had a similar experience a month later in June 2008 when I sailed into New York on the *Queen Mary II*. The trip was for our fortieth wedding anniversary. When we disembarked in New York, I handed my passport over. The official looked at his computer screen and looked at my passport. He looked at his computer screen again. Then he said his boss needed to speak to me. He called over his boss who said that two gentlemen from the FBI would like to speak to me. I was taken round the back. There were two men with a huge pile of paper. I told them that they knew this was all rubbish. I was the guy who was fixing the problem. They said they were sorry but they could not get into that. But they had to serve me "with this". It was a grand jury subpoena. I took it and went off and had a few days in New York. I then went to a board meeting in Washington where I gave my subpoena to Philip. I knew we could not comply with the subpoena. If we gave any written or oral evidence to the United States Government, we ran the real risk of being prosecuted by the UK government under the Official Secrets Act.[15]

This was the Kafkaesque aspect of the whole affair. We could not present evidence negating the charges because nobody was allowed to give a word of evidence. It was the most extraordinary case.

## 26. THREATS AND OPPORTUNITIES ABROAD

While we were dealing with our reputation in the US, it was already becoming apparent that we had regained a level of official acceptability in the UK. I had been asked to join Gordon Brown's Business Council for Britain, which he formed after he became prime minister in June 2007. The Labour party's fixer for business, Shriti Vadera, was always hovering around. She dealt with matters of substance but I always felt she helped Gordon deal with people skills. In November 2008 I joined a mission he was leading to some of the most important markets in the Middle East: Saudi Arabia, Qatar and the UAE. I would be hard pressed to say it was worthwhile. Little came of it, but then I had no expectations. It would have looked very strange if I had not gone. Saudi Arabia was our largest market after the US and UK. We had 5,000 employees there.

Ten days later I was back again, this time on purely BAE business. I spent a day in Saudi Arabia, my first visit there on BAE business since becoming chairman. Then I went on to Oman, for a meeting of the board. It was a fantastic visit. BAE was a big player in Oman: we had something like 70% share of the market. Oman was the first place the board[16] had met outside the UK or the US, certainly in my time. I do not think it would have happened under the former leadership of the company.

The board meeting was made possible by a trip I had made to Oman more than two years before. I had flown there directly from Moscow after a meeting with TNK-BP. I was in Muscat for a few days part work and part holiday with my family. I went to meet the head of the royal office, the Sultan's right-hand man. He had his interpreter there who translated my words into Arabic and his words into English. The conversation was getting deeper and deeper into regional issues. I told him I had met George Bush recently in Washington when we had discussed what the US was thinking about Iran. I told the president this might be best left to Yahoo. Meaning, there was another way to deal with Iran. Making sure that young people in Iran had access to the internet and wanted to join the world community. It would be more effective than firing rockets at them.

The head of the royal office told the interpreter to leave the room and go and do something. When we were alone he turned to me and said in perfect English he had just asked the Brigadier to go and prepare the war room. He took me into a room with wall-to-wall television screens all around. He told me he just wanted to show me what he thought might happen if the Americans were to take aggressive action against Iran. The

Omanis would be on the receiving end of any Iranian response. Iran was a big issue for them.

On that earlier visit there I also met Dr. Omar Zawawi. He was not the actual foreign minister, although he was the main adviser to the Sultan on foreign affairs. He was also on the Sultan's Privy Council. We met in the diwan, or Sultan's office, when I was seeing the head of the royal office and he invited me to dinner. He had the most stunning house set in a spectacular estate on the seafront. It had huge doors from floor to ceiling that were opened by beautiful women. Wonderful white jasmine perfumed the air. He had the finance minister and several other prominent people there. There was the most unbelievable red wine. I am not a red wine drinker: it gives me migraine. But I looked at the label: it was a vintage Margaux. I just had to taste it. I did and I did not get a headache. It must have been of exceptional quality.

At some point, we were talking about the Middle East and geopolitics. He asked me if I had read *Churchill's Folly*. I said I had not. So he leapt up from the dinner table, disappeared through the doors the women opened for him, and came back with a copy of the book, which he gave me. I still have it. It was about the decisions that Churchill made at the 1921 Cairo Conference. He sent one of the sons of the Hashemite Sharif of Mecca to be King of Iraq and another son to be ruler of Transjordan. The region is living with the consequences of his decisions to this day. It was getting late but then he said I should bring the board to dinner.

This is exactly what I did. It was to take more than two years to arrange but we had this amazing dinner, thanks to Dr Zawawi. Somebody was on a piano. It was quite unlike any board dinner we had ever had anywhere else.

CHAPTER 27

# Board Changes

THE BOARD BY this stage had changed radically, and in my view strengthened. To Sir Peter Mason, Michael Hartnall, Phil Carroll, Roberto Quarta and Sir Nigel Rudd we had added three more non-executive directors to provide a broader range of expertise. I was delighted to bring onto the board Andy Inglis, who was still at BP. I had of course known him a long time. Even so, he was much younger than most of the other people on the board. I thought the board would benefit from having a serving executive director. He was very able. Above all he was a huge performance guy, a real AAA personality. He was terrific on the board. He was on the corporate responsibility committee and he knew what he was doing. A further addition was Carl Symon, another American who had considerable experience in the UK. He was to chair the remuneration committee. Ravi Uppal joined at the same time, bringing his experience and expertise from the huge global powerhouse of India.

At the same time as I was constructing the board of BAE I was giving up my longest serving board position at Reuters. I had joined the board in December 1997. I had served beyond the maximum generally permitted nine years. I had been chairman of the audit committee during Sir Christopher Hogg's tenure as chairman; and I was senior independent director when Niall FitzGerald took over. I was all set to leave after ten years when Niall asked me to stay on to provide some continuity after the merger with Thomson. I told him I would be happy to stay on, but only for another year. The American directors could never understand why we limited our tenure: many served on boards in the US for years and years. That was a difference in corporate governance in the two countries.

BUILDING BRIDGES

Approaching 2010, I was coming up for my six years as chairman of BAE. I of course was subject to the six-year renewal conditions under the guidelines on governance like any other non-executive director. I fully supported those guidelines. There were briefings to the press that shareholders wanted me to move on. I knew this was not the case. I had reason to suspect that the briefing came from within the company or the board. I decided to try to flush the leaker out. We had a dinner of non-executive directors at the downstairs restaurant at the Dorchester. The place was like a dungeon. I told the board what I thought had happened and waited to see their reaction. I had my suspicions – but not enough to act on.

Within the business at BAE there followed another series of changes. I was worrying about where growth was going to come from when people stopped cutting steel and building ships. I thought we needed to move into other areas. Selling not only kit and platforms but also services. The acquisition of Detica, a cybersecurity company, marked out a new path. I still thought we would have a good future in unmanned aerial vehicles and so on. But cybersecurity was definitely going to be huge.

The core part of our business remained ships, aircraft and land vehicles. And in 2009 we had yet another twist to the carrier project. The ministry of defence announced that they were going to dump the F-35B jump-jet option of the Joint Strike Fighter and go for the F-35C carrier variant which had no short take-off and landing ability. This would require a reconfiguration of the take-off deck. The decision was announced days after construction started on the first carrier. This however would not be the end of the story.[17]

CHAPTER 28

# *Settlements*

WHILE THE JOINT Strike Fighter was of course an example of transatlantic collaboration, we were still having issues with the US Department of Justice. The reality was that in the case of a defence company, all contracts were with the government. If they took you to court and found you guilty of corruption, you could be barred from working with them again. You could lose half the company – or more. The challenge from the US posed an existential threat to the company. A fine of the amount that some people were talking about would have put the company out of business. It would have spelt the end to the company as we knew it. There were no doubt US competitor companies that would have gladly seen the demise of BAE. However it would have been in the interests of neither the UK nor the US for this to happen. We were one of the largest defence contractors for the United States. And it did not happen.

The fine was eventually fixed at $400 million. In 2010 we agreed to fines in both the US and the UK. This was not an admission that the company was guilty of corruption. Indeed the plea agreements did not charge BAE with bribery or authorising the payment of bribes. Rather BAE was charged with accounting irregularities. However we could not defend ourselves. We were not allowed by the UK authorities to give any evidence to a US Grand Jury or court.[18] Any more than a US corporation would be permitted to disclose US classified information to a non-US court. What the UK government did was not exceptional. Every sovereign state would do the same. It drew a red line. We could not contest the case. We would have to settle if we were to continue in business.

Before we settled with the Department of Justice and the SFO, I had gone to see David Cameron. I do not think I had ever met him before. He was then the leader of the opposition but it was likely he would lead the next government after the 2010 election. I told him I wanted to talk to him about Al-Yamamah. He called in Ken Clarke, the heavyweight former Chancellor who was shadow business secretary and was to be made Minister of Justice in the new Conservative government. I told them we were about to settle with the US Department of Justice. But I told them, the SFO was a problem to deal with. David Cameron needed to understand that the government was intimately involved with Al-Yamamah. "People in glass houses should not throw stones", I warned. So when this came up while they were in opposition, it was not an item to exploit. They should all lie down and keep quiet and we would take the flak. Then Ken asked about the SFO. I told them we were working with the SFO every day. I could not promise them that we would be able to do it but we were doing everything we could. The penny dropped. He guessed they might have to instruct the Attorney General to intervene with the SFO. I took this to mean that he hoped we could settle with the SFO so the new government would not have to act.

As part of any settlement, the Department of Justice would give you a monitor. Barclays and HSBC, and many other British companies, not only had to pay the monitor but the huge staff the monitors took on, sometimes hundreds of people. DoJ knew we were doing all the right things, so they could not give us instructions very easily, but they had to give us a monitor. We paid the $400 million fine and we said, the monitor had to be a UK person because of all the UK eyes only requirements. Philip started sending names to the Department of Justice. He had sent four names. In every case we had been told, no. Then he sent a fifth name. This one was accepted by the Department of Justice. The fifth name that went to the Department of Justice was David Gold. He was senior partner at Herbert Smith lawyers, experts in white collar crime. The DoJ accepted his nomination. He became the monitor. He had no staff. We again gave him free access to the whole company, the board and particularly the corporate responsibility committee. We told him we knew what we were doing but continuous improvement would be great. He was fantastic. Most people talk of monitors as being a problem. Our monitor was I believe very challenging but incredibly constructive and really helpful. We taught him everything he knows about being a monitor. When eventually

## 28. SETTLEMENTS

he had to leave at the end of his stint monitoring BAE, he was in great demand. He went on to advise Rolls-Royce, Airbus and others.

The Department of Justice was not the only arm of the US government that was gunning for BAE. Not to be outdone, the US State Department issued proceedings against us. They were the department responsible for enforcing the Arms Export Control Act and the International Traffic in Arms Regulations, two US instruments to restrict and control the export of defence equipment and military technology. Defence companies were meant to monitor their own activities and then send regular reports to Washington. We had failed to send any reports on any payment to agents. So a year after the DoJ fined us $400m, we reached a civil settlement with the State Department for a penalty of $49m, the largest civil penalty ever paid to it. We also agreed to the presence of a monitor to ensure future compliance reporting.

We continued what we had started. We made each member of the corporate responsibility committee, each independent director that was a member – we had three of them – responsible for one area. One had diversity and inclusion, one had ethics, and one had safety. We actually made an independent director responsible for making sure this stayed alive. For this was an issue that really should never go away. We should be making constant improvement. Even in the little things, there should be zero tolerance of breaches of ethical standards.

There remained outstanding issues with the SFO. It was all agreed with its director Richard Alderman at a meeting at four in the morning after Philip came back from the US. We announced the settlements with the DoJ and SFO simultaneously. We did not accept we had behaved improperly in securing a contract for a radar system with Tanzania. We did however admit to a minor accounting error. In the end we suggested to them that we plead guilty to failing properly to account for a payment. We would go to court that would determine any fine we needed to pay for contravening the law. So in December 2010, BAE appeared before a court on one charge of accounting irregularities under the 1985 Companies Act. We had not correctly recorded the payments to an agent in Tanzania who was selling them a radar for £28m. The judge fined us £500,000.

We agreed to pay a penalty of £30m in the context of the SFO settlement. We paid the fine and would pay the balance of the £30m to the people of Tanzania. Philip told me we then had to go to the SFO to record the settlement. They accepted it. That left £29,500,000. This was a lot of money. We wanted to make a real difference in Tanzania. We needed to talk to people who really understood Africa in general and Tanzania in particular on how to do this. Philip started to put together a team who had insight and experience in how we could do it. They considered making a real difference by educating young people or providing fresh water or sanitation. We had a high-level team of experts looking at wise, sensible and practical options. The committee was led by Earl Cairns, a former banker who had been head of VSO and also CDC – the main development finance body for the UK government.

There was some wrangling with the government about where the money should go and should not go. We felt we had been rather thoughtful about how the money should be allocated and disbursed. We thought we should make sure this money would not go on Mercedes limousines or private jets for the President. Rather it should go to the people of Tanzania in a way that had some enduring benefit. We agreed a system where it could be done and audited by us. It still took months and months negotiating how it was going to be done. It was not until March 2012 that the money was actually handed over to Tanzania. As for the radar it is similar to the one functioning at Gatwick airport and was sold for close to the same price. For anyone with past experience of flying into Tanzania airport, the radar provides some reassurance of a safer landing.

CHAPTER 29

# Working for Britain

THERE WERE OTHER signs that the world had noticed that I was changing BAE from the top down. After being on Gordon Brown's Business Council for Britain, I was with David Cameron for five years on his Business Advisory Group. It was the same membership serving the same purpose with a different party in power. We had gone from being pariahs as a company to being close to the government of the day, as we should be. We had very close relationships with senior officials like Jonathan Powell, Gus O'Donnell and Jeremy Heywood. At the same time we had good and useful relations with the succession of prime ministers, both Labour and Conservative: Tony Blair, Gordon Brown and David Cameron. Not that we always agreed with the government's decisions. On assuming power in 2010, David Cameron commissioned a strategic defence and security review. As a result, the government cancelled the programme to upgrade the Nimrod maritime surveillance aircraft. I thought this a great pity, having rebuilt the whole thing and having spent around £3 billion by the time it was cancelled.

In addition to BAE, and the prime minister's Business Advisory Group, across at Carlton House Terrace at the Royal Academy of Engineering I also chaired the panel on Education For Engineers – E4E. Being engaged with those three enterprises made it possible to achieve things. Governments might have been well-meaning but they needed guidance. One of their less well thought through initiatives was to scrap the design and technology curriculum in England and Wales for 14-18 year olds and promote a different approach. Their new ideas were better suited for a bygone era.

A previous government had put in place diplomas from hairdressing to engineering. The engineering one had been worked on really hard by the Royal Academy of Engineering and by companies that needed trained engineers. We knew what we wanted. We trained the teachers to teach what we needed. The diploma required four GSCEs for which a huge amount of content was produced.

Then the secretary of education Michael Gove decided with the stroke of his pen to get rid of this carefully devised curriculum.

At the time I spoke out publicly against the minister's proposals for a rejigged national design and technology curriculum. It would teach children more about horticulture and cookery than about technology. I laid out my misgivings to a conference of teachers. I said that the proposed curriculum changes did

> not meet the needs of a technologically literate society. Instead of introducing children to new design techniques, such as biomimicry (how we can emulate nature to solve human problems), we now have a focus on cookery. Instead of developing skills in computer-aided design, we have the introduction of horticulture. Instead of electronics and control, we have an emphasis on basic mechanical maintenance tasks. In short, something has gone very wrong.

BAE Systems had already demonstrated its commitment to training technicians for the future. We had hundreds of apprentices in our businesses. I was not alone in voicing my considerable disquiet and annoyance at the government's proposal. The engineer and designer of so many household appliances Sir James Dyson said of the proposed changes: "This new curriculum will not inspire the inventors and engineers Britain so desperately needs. The academic rigour Mr Gove demanded in other core subjects is missing in Design and Technology."

In response to my public criticisms of the proposed curriculum changes the Parliamentary Under-Secretary of State at the Department for Education, one Elizabeth Truss, invited the Royal Academy of Engineering and other interested parties to re-draft the curriculum. We had only a matter of days to do this. I pointed out that the government's proposals were inadequate for preparing teenagers in our country for design and technology in the generation to come. I offered to take the pen away and we would re-write the curriculum to cover twenty-first century science engineering and materials. She accepted that. But then she said something really extraordinary. It was scarcely believable. She said, as long as we

## 29. WORKING FOR BRITAIN

supported mathematics. I told her there was absolutely no question about that. Her question was all the more shocking given that her father was a professor of maths. She herself had got into Oxford on maths: she then switched to Philosophy, Politics and Economics. I reassured her we were fully behind all of the STEM subjects: science, technology, engineering *and* mathematics. We thought it was important for the country and the economy.

She buckled to our wishes – but she insisted on including cooking in our syllabus. The question was where to include it – so she foisted it on D&T.

This is how the government explained the decision:

> As part of their work with food, pupils should be taught how to cook and apply the principles of nutrition and healthy eating. Instilling a love of cooking in pupils will also open a door to one of the great expressions of human creativity. Learning how to cook is a crucial life skill that enables pupils to feed themselves and others affordably and well, now and in later life.
>
> [From the government national curriculum for Design and Technology September 2013]

Even if we all agreed with that, why should it be part of the curriculum to train up the next generation of skilled engineers and technicians for the needs of industry? My next concern was about the engineering diploma.

I tried to see the minister, wearing my three hats from BAE, the Royal Academy of Engineering, and the prime minister's Business Advisory Group. Michael Gove would not see me. Until he was forced to.

I was at a meeting of a number of people from industry on the Business Advisory Group. David Cameron was always on time or nearly on time; for once he was not there yet. I was having a conversation about skills with Matt Hancock, the minister at BEIS (Business, Energy and Industrial Strategy). The Prime Minister came in. I told him I was talking to Matt about this problem but Gove would not speak to me. He turned to Matt and said, "Fix that".

The following day Janet got a call from Gove's office and I went to see him. He was very challenging and combative. He had a phalanx of people with him. I was in effect on my own. He just did not want to hear. But he had to. And finally he yielded. We also dealt with the computer science curriculum. There were diplomas for computer science, design and technology, and engineering. We got all three sorted out during the time I had these three hats. This achievement was noted in my citation for the President's Medal from the Royal Academy of Engineering.

The promotion of education was something I believed in more strongly than any other single issue for the betterment of society and the world we live in. It is what we should bequeath every generation. I was often flabbergasted how politicians, with their short-term vision, could be so dismissive of the imperative of investing in the young. I was invited by Shriti Vadera to a dinner in the West End with Ed Miliband, who was then leader of the opposition Labour Party. He had been minister for energy and climate change in the last two years of Gordon Brown's government. A number of other chairmen of FTSE 100 companies were there as well as the president of the Royal Academy of Engineering, Sir John Parker. Ed Miliband had two things on his mind that night. The first, which occupied most of the time, was that he wanted to put a cap on the price of electricity. That was to become topical in the energy crisis of 2022 but that was not the case back then. Every single chairman around the table, including me, said this really was not a very sensible idea. We needed more electric power. This required investment. And if you want investment you cannot put a cap on the price like that. His next question was how we were to close the gap between the country's rich and poor. Most of the other chairmen were exhausted by the earlier conversation. I decided that I had better give him an answer. I said he had asked a very good question, a very strategic question. And the answer was very strategic. It would not be achieved in 10 minutes. The answer was education. Which is, of course, what Tony Blair, used to say: "Education, education, education". I said education was the way to solve this problem. Give every child the best opportunity they can have. I will never forget his answer. He said, that might be necessary, but it was not sufficient. By which I assumed he meant, the best thing is to tax the rich and give to the poor. This obviously does not provide a very good, constructive base to teach people how to fish, rather than to give them fish. At that moment Shriti's telephone rang, with the news that Mandela had died (it was 5 December 2013). And that was the end of the dinner.

I have said that what BAE sold was not only defence equipment but also a relationship with the British government. This pitch did not always work. One deal that slipped from us at the last minute was in the Middle East. We were convinced it was going to happen. We had sold, we thought,

## 29. WORKING FOR BRITAIN

24 or a possible 48 Typhoons to the UAE. Every one of the 3,000 pages of the contract had been initialled by all sides. I had organised for the prime minister David Cameron to land in Abu Dhabi and sign it. Shaikh Muhammad bin Zayed, by then Crown Prince and defence minister and to all intents and purposes the main force in the Emirates, decided that morning that he would not sign it. David Cameron actually had his wheels on the ground. He was incredibly helpful – but even his presence did not sway the Emiratis.

Another time we were all on the prime minister's 747 with David Cameron on our way to India. We landed at some ungodly hour of the night. Negotiations with the Indians had been going on for years. We were never certain that they would actually sign.[19] We were keen as were the prime minister and his team that there should be no hitch. We all spoke to our opposite numbers to insist that we *were* signing this thing. There were comings and goings and messages backwards and forwards. This went on until about an hour before the pen was got out and we actually signed in Bangalore, where the aircraft were going to be built under license.

The long serving prime minister of India Manmohan Singh was one of the most impressive world leaders I ever met. I was struck above all by his humanity. He was meeting probably 50 of us for a hastily put together state banquet for David Cameron. Yet he was somebody who had time for each and every one of us. He looked me in the eyes. He shook hands and then held my hand with his other hand. It was very interesting. Here was a serious person, wanting to take note of everything I said. (Another person who had the same aura was Bill Clinton. Everyone said the same. I only met him once, at Davos. But he fixed me with his eyes for ten minutes and gave me his undivided attention. He made me feel that there was nobody else and nothing else that he was interested in but me.)

In 2012 we held our first board meeting in Saudi Arabia, in recognition of its importance to us as a major customer. I had always held that to be effective, directors needed to have a proper understanding of the business. By that time we had shuffled the board some more. Andy Inglis and Phil Carroll had left in 2010. Phil was in my opinion the best non-executive director BAE had in my time. But he said after he had been with us less than five years that he felt the time had come when he should leave. When I asked him why, he said he was not as sharp as he used to be (he died four years later). Roberto Quarta and Ravi Uppal left in 2011. We brought in

Paul Anderson, from the energy industry in the US, a big guy in all respects (he later became a non-executive director at BP); Lee McIntire who knew our sort of business extremely well; Nick Rose, who was the CFO of Diageo and who chaired our Audit Committee and later became the senior independent director; and Paula Rosput Reynolds, who was absolutely fabulous. She was a terrific person and had had a fantastic career in both the US and the UK. She was someone who really understood business. She worked hard at it. She wanted to know the detail. And she was a good judge of people and became senior independent director of BP and chair of National Grid.

This was the first visit for many of them to one of our most important clients. They were able to go out and meet some of our employees and get an idea of what our contribution was to Saudi Arabia. We also were able to receive feedback from senior Saudi officials about how they judged our performance. We went to an Air Force site and saw the aircraft being used, really being used, and probably being used more than the ones in the UK. It felt more serious. It felt more like we were near the action. The Saudi military were completely unfazed by the sight of our three female board members – Linda Hudson, an executive director and two non-executives, Harriet Green and Paula Rosput Reynolds – clambering into aircraft cockpits. We sent them to meet the first 15 women working for BAE in Saudi Arabia. They were probably the first Saudi women to work in the defence industry. BAE had asked them whether they wanted to work by themselves, or whether they wanted to work with other parts of the company. And they said they would really quite like to work together. This in a country where at the time women were not allowed to drive on public roads. I asked our women directors about them and they said they were really enjoying themselves. They had a row of hooks, where they would hang up their abayas. And underneath they would be wearing the absolute latest European fashions.

On a previous trade mission with Gordon Brown I had been put up in the Four Seasons. BAE being BAE ensured I spent the night in a bunker behind a six-foot thick concrete wall. In Saudi Arabia they were conscious of the bomb attacks on compounds housing western residents a couple of years before.

I had a fascinating hour with Prince Salman, the Crown Prince and defence minister. With me I had Sir Sherard Cowper-Coles, who of course

## 29. WORKING FOR BRITAIN

knew the kingdom well from his time there. He had joined BAE as an adviser the previous year after leaving the diplomatic service. We were getting along so well, with Prince Salman wanting to talk about his house in Spain. The serried ranks of generals on the far side of the room were clearly getting uncomfortable! A message was passed to the Crown Prince. He turned to me and said how important it was to keep costs under control and to maintain efficiency, which I clearly agreed with. At one point Sherard jumped in to correct the interpreter who had misinterpreted what I was saying. A wonderful man to have with you in Saudi Arabia!

Saudi Arabia had long been our most important export market. We were now looking at a move that could be a significant game changer for the company.

CHAPTER 30

# *The Biggest Defence Company?*

IN ONE OF those strategy sessions another far more ambitious project came up, one that could transform the company and the industry. Tim Shacklock, from Gleacher Shacklock, boutique banker, and I were always talking about it. When I first got to BAE, Tim was already an adviser. He had been an adviser for many years to the BAE executive. The one project that he and I used to talk about all the time was whether we should merge with EADS, the largest European aerospace conglomerate. The issue came up again almost at the end of my ten years at BAE. The timing seemed right for a merger.

The strategic reasoning was obvious. It would combine Europe's two biggest aerospace companies to create the largest in the world, to take on the Americans. It would bring together BAE's strengths in the defence sector with EADS's conglomeration of successful commercial companies. EADS also had a defence sector, but its outstanding asset was Airbus. For years, Airbus and Boeing had been in a dogfight to dominate the commercial aircraft market. Airline fleets across the world were – and still are – made up almost exclusively of their jetliners. Both sides would benefit. EADS thanks to BAE would gain a bigger foothold in the United States for its defence and security business. BAE was already the largest European defence contractor and the US was its largest market. BAE would be part of a group once more that built commercial aircraft.

The two companies knew each other well. We had worked together on different projects and products. These included the Typhoon (Eurofighter) – Airbus was one of the partners – and Airbus commercial aircraft as well as missiles.

In terms of scale, the two companies together would be bigger than

## 30. THE BIGGEST DEFENCE COMPANY?

the competition. It would be combining EADS that had annual revenue (for 2011) of nearly £40bn to BAE's just under £20bn. Together at £58 bn we would have been larger than any of the US companies.

We examined the exchange ratios and felt a merger was right rather than an acquisition by one of the other. When we approached EADS, they were willing partners. I had known Tom Enders, the German chief executive of EADS, for years: I had appointed him to BP AG thirty years before.

However the chairman of EADS was from the Lagardère family. It owned Hachette and other media interests as well as a large chunk of EADS. The French wanted to preserve the status quo in the French military industrial complex. This made the chairman basically conflicted in any sale. So EADS appointed Sir John Parker and the steel magnate Lakshmi Mittal as the two non-executive directors of EADS to negotiate with me. We were to decide who was to get what job and who was going to do what. I went to Lakshmi Mittal's huge house in Kensington Palace Gardens, colloquially known as 'embassy row', near Len Blavatnik's magnificent mansion. We were given tea and cakes with gold leaf on them. I had never had cake with gold leaf on it before.

As in any deal we had to decide on all the social issues: who was going to be chair, who was going to be chief executive, who was going to be chief executive of the defence business, who was going to chair each of the board committees, the balance of Europeans and Americans on the board, who was going to be on the board and who was not. These issues had to be discussed and agreed for all those key positions. Quite apart from the commercial issues. Usually there is a commercial issue or a social issue so nothing happens. And then if the commercial issues are agreed, often deals fall through because of some social issue. Quite often these things do not happen because nobody can agree to step down. We had also ringfenced nuclear defence, under special security agreements.

Furthermore the British government supported us. The defence secretary Philip Hammond, who was opinionated but able, was behind us. The prime minister David Cameron was with us. There were voices of opposition to us in the US: mainly leaks from concerned rival US companies. But the Pentagon and the White House were for us. We might have had problems in the US but it never got that far.

We had good reason to believe that the Pentagon would welcome us.

143

They saw us as a disruptor, to stir things up with the main US contractors Boeing, McDonnell Douglas, Lockheed Martin and Raytheon. A new competitor would help the Pentagon challenge these companies on quality and price. The Pentagon wanted the strongest possible counterparty to the US industrial giants. Pentagon policy had always paid for the luxury of not depending on a single source. It was costly, but it created greater security. The Pentagon also wanted the European members of Nato to pay for a greater share of their own defence. A bigger European defence contractor should make that more likely.

We had been working in secret for about 11 weeks. In August we decided to have a week's break. Tom Enders said he looked forward to going skydiving. Some of us questioned whether this was a wise idea. He dismissed the concern: he had done 2,000 dives. After our minibreak we met in some dingy old airfield. Our team arrived in a lumbering old BAe 125. The delegation from Airbus screamed onto the airstrip in a sleek top-of-the-range Falcon 7x. The aircraft door swung open, and at the top of the steps we saw Tom. His right arm was sticking out in front of him. On his last dive he had hit the ground at 60 knots, smashed his shoulder and ripped his arm away from the rib cage. He was in a body brace, stapled through the skin. We could see he was in immense pain. Beads of sweat appeared on his forehead. But he kept going throughout the meeting, without missing a beat.

Tom Enders was in charge of dealing with German Chancellor Angela Merkel. He was a straight talker: he was a major in the German army reserve, a former paratrooper. When he approached her, she told him, if he wanted to speak now, the answer was no. She was too busy trying to save the euro and bailing out Greece. We could not choose the timing. There was no one around her who was willing or able to state that what we were proposing was a once in a lifetime move that would have transformed the European aerospace sector forever. As was widely reported, there was disagreement over where the various headquarters of the different business should be. This was not a dealbreaker. It showed many in positions of authority understood very little of the opportunity they were failing to grasp.

Tom probably did not have a chance. He was not used to dealing with Berlin. Whatever the message, he was not the messenger they were open to. He may have been the wrong kind of German. He was from West

## 30. THE BIGGEST DEFENCE COMPANY?

Germany. Mrs Merkel and some of her closest advisers were from East Germany. More of an issue is that many of the Green party she had made a coalition with were against any form of defence industry. External factors were against us.

We had a meeting with the French parties in Airbus. We explained that we had to keep the talks confidential. Under UK rules, once a plan for a merger had been announced, we had a limited number of days to conclude the deal. It was a question of transparency. We had to put up or shut up. The French could understand neither the idiom nor the concept. We asked them how long it took after we informed the president or defence minister before the fact we were in merger talks would be leaked. Given the politicised nature of the French civil service, they said, maximum of eight hours. Probably five. The news was indeed leaked – from France, according to the FT.

We had the backing of the US, UK and French governments even before we were forced to announce our merger plans. It was on 12 September 2012 that BAE and EADS made their intentions public. BAE shareholders would own 40% of the merged group; EADS shareholders 60%. The announcement of the intention to merge set the clock running on the 28-day period in which to finalise the deal.

I firmly believe the merger collapsed because Angela Merkel simply said no. She said she did not want it. I do not think we spent enough time trying to convince the Chancellor of the advantages of the tie-up. I also wonder whether her view might have been: As Germany, did they really want to have the largest defence company in the world? It was the third disastrous decision she took after deciding not to have nuclear power and determining that the Russians were a reliable supplier of gas.

There were reports in the press that it was shareholders opposed to the merger who had scuppered the plan. That is nonsense. It was one person and one person only who stopped it. That was Mrs Merkel. I felt, and the board felt, that the merger was a great idea. But once she said no, there was nothing we could do.

Invesco, the largest shareholder in BAE, stated publicly that the deal would not be good for shareholders. It would not have been good for their former star fund manager Neil Woodford. He would not have got an uplift because there was no premium paid: it was a straight merger, so no shares were bought or sold. However within just over ten years BAE's share price had gone from £3.12 in September 2012 to £8.54 in February 2023 and over £13 in July 2024; EADS shot from 25.70 euros to 116 euros in the same period. Shareholders would have done very well in the combined company.

Had it happened, it would have been the most successful and powerful aerospace and defence company in the world. It would have been bigger and better in almost every respect than Boeing. It was an opportunity missed. And it could not happen now, in the post-Brexit world.

CHAPTER 31

# Stepping Down

In 2013, I received a letter informing me that I was being awarded a knighthood. I was not to tell anybody. I had known it was in the works. I had been told many people had been recommending me for this honour for some time. I had already won a number of industry awards, such as the NED of the year award in 2011. That was the recognition by my peers. Most chairmen of leading UK companies were knighted. However I was told there was an obstacle. A very considerable obstacle. I had basically been blackballed.

The story went back nearly twenty years, to my time at BP. In the nineties I had been put forward for a knighthood for my work in the Gulf of Mexico. I was reliably informed that the nominations committee however received an objection to this from none other than BP itself. I had known nothing about this: either the recommendation, or that someone in BP had been so against me being honoured that they made a formal objection to it. The trouble with the system is that once you have such an objection against your name – and I do not know what the grounds were – it is difficult to remove the stain. That despite the growing clamour from my peers against what they considered the injustice after all I had done at BAE that I had not received wider recognition.

I know at least one person who wrote to the Prime Minister and the Cabinet Secretary asking what the hell was going on. After I got the offer letter I had a word with Jeremy Heywood. He said they had broken every rule in the book to get this done. I took that to mean over the earlier blackball. There could have been another issue. I had been an investor in a film production company, Ingenious Films. HMRC thought this was a tax avoidance scheme. I paid the tax due – because I did not want anything hanging over my heirs – and pulled out of the film production company, but this was after my knighthood.

So John Browne's prediction that by joining BAE I would get a knighthood turned out to be correct, though it took nearly a decade.

As I was leaving BAE I was summoned to Buckingham Palace for tea with Prince Andrew, the Duke of York. He wanted to thank me for all my good work at BAE. There had been scepticism within the company about how much value he added as Business Ambassador, particularly in the Middle East. Critics said he was always going off message. I had to remind them that he would gain access to foreign princes and shaikhs and they could not. We would agree to give him a brief on a single issue.

I left BAE on 1 February 2014, just short of ten years since it was announced I was to become chairman. I had wanted a challenge and I certainly had one. It was a much bigger challenge than I had ever imagined it would be. I faced a real personal crisis in my early confrontations with the old guard. And the company also faced difficult times, much of their own making.

The period of the SFO and DoJ enquiries was a very unsettling time. Employees were questioned under caution. Premises were raided. The press was hostile. Our share price plummeted. The DoJ enquiry could have broken the company. It certainly was a wake-up call. The old school approach was to tough it out. I felt, as did my allies on the board, that we needed a root and branch transformation of the company and its culture.

That was a disturbing coda to the SFO affair. Some years after the SFO closed its investigation into BAE it admitted that thousands of confidential documents had gone missing. They only realised they had been sent to the wrong address a year after the event. Some ended up in a disused marijuana farm in the east end of London.[20] Others had been delivered in error to one of the witnesses in the case.

What I learnt above all in my years in business was to remain true to what I knew to be right. That might sound arrogant for someone who the former chief executive of BAE dismissed as not knowing anything about the industry. But sometimes it helps to have an outsider looking in. That is why under the rules of governance, emphasis is placed on the independence of non-executive directors. These must form the majority. I and my other independent directors – though as chairman I was not classed as independent – brought a different perspective to the board.

## 31. STEPPING DOWN

We had had huge collective experience of business and finance, running companies and dealing with governments around the world.

I knew from the moment I entered Stirling Square that the place needed to be dragged into the twenty-first century. The company might be making state of the art technology and leading-edge machines. But the way it operated was of another era. This was not sustainable. My objective was to change the culture of the company, and its governance, while maintaining and expanding its industrial excellence.

The launch of the SFO enquiry underlined in my eyes the need for change. It is no secret that not everyone on the board was persuaded that the company needed to change. But as an engineer, I was trained to solve problems, step by step. It meant analysing the problem to devise the solution. I could change my ideas, so the board would accept me. That would mean yielding on everything that I knew to be correct. The alternative was to make the board more amenable. That was a two-stage process. First, to take out the dead wood, the lifers, those who had become too cosy with the executive, who were no longer independent – if indeed they ever had been. The next stage towards creating a world-class board was to shift the balance. Executives would be a minority on the board. That after all was as stipulated by the Combined Code – and had been recognised by the board (see 2003 Annual Report).

It took six years for the enterprise to be turned round. That required from me steadfastness of purpose, an inner conviction and clarity of what needed to be done. And then a certain resolve to ensure that it was. It was a hugely risky task for me personally. I would not have missed it for the world.

This decade had been a wonderful example of the need for leaders to do what is right irrespective of all the personal risks that that might attract. To create real change takes perseverance, determination, and a willingness to risk one's job and many other things. To make real change is risky, but needs to be done. Rarely is change or doing the right thing popular. Perhaps politicians should think more about that. When I left the company, the value of the enterprise was nearly three times more than what it had been when I joined. Change is also good economically.

There were those who derided our insistence on doing everything we did to the highest possible standards of business behaviour. They said we would lose business to other less scrupulous providers of defence equipment and services. They were right. We did lose some markets – of our own choosing. We felt we were unable and unwilling to operate or make deals in certain jurisdictions. We may have walked away from business. We were simply not prepared to work with them. The markets were too toxic,[21] too systemically corrupt. And our decision did not always go down well with the UK authorities. HMG was particularly upset about the impact on bilateral relations when we gave up on certain deals. However other markets opened up to us. In 2012 we had sold more outside the US and UK than any time in history. That is why I told shareholders the new culture of the firm would become a strong competitive advantage. Some customers who might have been put off by the enquiries into our past conduct were reassured by and attracted by our very clearly stated reform of our business culture. These included customers in the Middle East. When King Abdullah ruled that there should be no more role for intermediaries in Saudi government contracts, we had already moved to work in that way. We concluded an initial deal for Typhoon in 2005 and a second deal in 2018, after I had left. We were more competitive than before.

The thing I am most proud of is that in the decade since I left in 2014 there has been no resumption of the earlier press frenzy. The whole company is more thoughtful. It has changed radically from the 2004 company I walked into. Ten years after I left, it is run by a superb chair, excellent executive and a super talented workforce of wonderful engineers and highly skilled workers from other disciplines. In today's world we need them than more than at any time in the past eight decades.

23. With another kind of vessel, after jumping ship to BAE.

24. The SFO announced an investigation into the sale of a radar to Tanzania [page 133]. The cartoon exaggerates the damage: we were largely unscathed.

25. I had cleaned up the culture of BAE. But I still had to deal with legacy issues.

26. Preparing for a flight in a Typhoon fighter.

27. The cartoon rightly shows the EADS deal was shot down by Angela Merkel [page 145].

28. With Bill Clinton at Davos, when I was at BAE [page 139].

29. With Prime Minister David Cameron in India, selling Hawk aircraft [page 139].

30. With Prime Minister Tony Blair and President Jacques Chirac at the unveiling of the Airbus A380 in Toulouse, 18 January 2005.

31. With President George W Bush.

32. With Vice President Dick Cheney.

33. With Her Majesty Queen Elizabeth II [page 119].

34. With King Salman of Saudi Arabia [page 140].

To Pamela and Dick Olver
With best wishes,

35. Pam and me with President George W and Laura Bush.

36. Coming up for air....through the hatch of an Astute-class submarine.

37. In Nimrod before Cameron cancelled the programme.

CHAPTER 32

# Retirement? What retirement?

WHEN I LEFT BAE I was 67. I had wanted another job as chairman. RTZ had not worked because of timing. And my hopes of heading up Europe's largest defence contractor were shot down by Mrs Merkel. How could I match the experience I had had at BP? And the BAE experience, even with all its tumultuous problems, was probably the most interesting chairman's job in London. It was going to be very difficult to do anything comparable.

I was fortunate that several years before leaving BAE I had a meeting that would provide a solution. I was approached by Luke Meynell of the executive search firm Russell Reynolds. He had been charged by HSBC with finding a senior adviser in the UK. At the time I was sitting on David Cameron's business advisory group. The only member from the financial services sector was the chairman of HSBC, Stephen Green (soon to be Lord Green). I knew him quite well. I asked what this was about. He had the same Rolodex as I had. He asked me to come and have lunch together with the chief executive, Stuart Gulliver. They said they just wanted somebody who could go and talk to chairmen and senior executives in London. I belonged to so many Chairmen's groups, sharing best practice. I challenged them. What could I do that they could not? They said they did not know. But they did not have sufficient time to cover the waterfront. They needed my help.

I am not sure that Stephen Green was the sort of person who would actually ask the client for business. I joined HSBC sometime around 2009 or 2010. Several other people had been recruited, including Stuart Rose (Lord Rose) from Marks and Spencer and Glen Moreno, chairman of Pearson. Initially we would meet with a whole range of European advisers from Portugal and Spain and France and Germany. One adviser, an American banker, asked why I was involved in so much stuff. I was engaged because I was interested and felt I could contribute. A lot of these advisers ended up going. One reason may have been they could not change gear. They had to realise that their value was in helping and mentoring young people in the organisation on the way up. They could enable these young people to get to a level with people outside the bank that they could not reach by themselves. For example, I helped a very able young banker in the resources section by introducing him to Andrew Gould, who was on the board of a company that the bank was interested in. I took Andrew to dinner and brought the young guy along. I was happy to make the introduction to help give the banker a leg up. After all, I had been given often unseen help and mentoring by senior people when I was on the way up in BP. I felt I was in a position, and had a certain obligation, to help a younger generation to benefit from what I had to offer. I saw my role as an enabler. Institutionally, HSBC should have senior people inside as well performing this function. However many large organisations are consumed with internal meetings and processes. As a result they might spend too little time dealing with people outside.

After some time, HSBC offered me the role of vice chairman. But I did not want an office in Canary Wharf. I did not want a job where I was on call 24/7. I told them I was happy with the senior advisory position. I felt I could continue to be of use to the management by being of help to younger staff and accessing the C suite of the world's companies. Somewhat surprisingly I still seemed able to do this a decade and more later.

In the years since leaving BAE, I have had very few conversations about defence. Almost all the work I have been asked to advise on taps into my expertise gained at BP. Even though I left BP in 2004, most of it has been about oil and gas resources, utilities, the energy transition, and mining. It was true that few of my contemporaries were still active in the industry. That did not mean I had no contacts of any consequence. The reality was that the people that I helped on their way up, as others had helped me, were now in senior positions all over the world.

People who retired from BP almost invariably were snapped up for top jobs in the same industry or elsewhere. John Buchanan was on five FTSE 100 boards. Chris Gibson-Smith ran the London Stock Exchange. Tony Hayward was chairman of Glencore. Andrew McKenzie became chairman

## 32. RETIREMENT? WHAT RETIREMENT?

of Shell. John Manzoni was president and CEO of Talisman in Canada; then chief executive of the UK civil service and cabinet office permanent secretary, chairman of SSE and chairman of Diageo. Tony Meggs became chairman of Crossrail after heading the infrastructure and projects authority. Paul Smith, one of my high potential guys, joined Wintershall Dea as CFO. Andy Hopwood, who used to be my chief of staff, became a non-Executive Director of Harbour Energy. Anne Drinkwater joined the board of Tullow, and then Equinor and Balfour Beatty. Brian Gilvary was chosen to run Ineos Energy; and Lamar Mckay became chairman of APA holdings, which in effect meant Apache, one of the largest independent oil and gas companies. I do not think that any other company has provided so many great executives to the world outside as BP.

As soon as I left BAE, Roberto Quarta got in touch. Roberto was a long standing operating partner of CD&R, the private equity firm. He told me they had room for me and Janet. What is more, the move could not have been more convenient. Their offices were in King Street, 100 yards from BAE's office. He suggested we wheel our chairs round the corner. Which we did a second time. It gave me an office in St James's which was invaluable. More importantly, they were incredibly good at what they did. When I started they were working on Fund Eight. They then did Nine, Ten, 11 and 12. I helped them where I could. For example, we merged MFG (Motor Fuel Group) with MRH, the U.K.'s largest petrol station and convenience retail operator. As a result we had about 900 fuel stations which made it the largest owner of fuel stations in the United Kingdom. I helped them when we were thinking of buying Exxon's assets in Germany although it never happened. I also felt I provided value for senior management: Dave Novak, co-president of the firm globally, told me he liked to be challenged.

There was no conflict between my advisory work with HSBC and my role at CD&R. There were times when CD&R might have been frustrated that HSBC had not acted quickly on some issue. Then I stepped in with a can of WD40 to ease relations between people and to build bridges.

I was approached once by Bob Maguire, who runs Carlyle's energy business to become an adviser. This would have been a great opportunity but I could not be adviser to two private equity firms.

However when Simon Eyers, the head of energy for Warburg Pincus in Europe came to see me, he did not want me to join Warburg Pincus:

153

that would not have been possible. He came with a proposal that would not be in conflict with my work for CD&R. They were looking for a non-Executive Director for a Dutch company to produce gas in Hungary and Romania. They asked me to join the advisory board – I later became chairman – of Sand Hill Petroleum. We had board meetings in Amsterdam. It was interesting. Later we recruited Jack Golden. With us were a couple of old BP hands: Martin Fossum, a petroleum engineer who had worked for BP in Russia and for TNK-BP, was the CEO; and Peter Nolan, an explorer from BP, who had worked a lot in North Africa and the Middle East, was also part of the business. We were doing conventional gas, looking at mature areas onshore, to see where the application of the most up-to-date technological approaches could find and develop overlooked resources. By 2015 the company was producing gas but the challenge was that the gas price was very low.

The trouble was they were behaving like a private equity firm. They wanted to load up the debt as soon as they could, rather than putting more equity in. So in 2018 we obtained a EUR 70 million bond on the Norwegian bond market. However when the gas price fell, the company could not service the loan and had no chance of repaying it and the interest, now $90m. The company ended up being owned by the debt holders, as often happened in the United States. I resigned at the end of 2021. And then of course, the Ukraine war came. The price of gas went up – but too late for us. It was all about timing. This was not the only small oil and gas investment I was involved in that did not end up well for me.

A little earlier a group of us formed a company called Edgewater to frack for oil in the Eagle Ford in southern Texas. I was a director along with several other excellent ex-BP people including Jack Golden, Scott Urban, Tim Holt and Larry McVay. We were having difficulty in finding a funder. I told them I could contact Goldman Sachs and see what happened. I called Julian Metherell, still at that time the oil and gas person at Goldmans. We were looking for $250 million. He asked who else was involved. There might be some conflict of interest over some consulting work some of his guys were doing. He said he would talk to New York and call me back. He called me back at seven o'clock the same evening to say they would do it. In the end Goldmans invested about $150 million. It was quite late to get into the Eagle Ford so after a short time we turned our attention to the gas fracking business called EdgeMarc in the

## 32. RETIREMENT? WHAT RETIREMENT?

Marcellus. The team had found an opportunity to access acreage. The gas price was very low. It was quite a tricky business. We were skewered by an event over which we had no control. The pipeline that we had contracted to take our gas fell off the side of a mountain. It would take a year to put it back, what with all the regulations to be complied with. Goldmans decided that they would not fund the company during that period. So they allowed the company to slip into bankruptcy. The company went into the hands of the debt holders. This is what has happened a hundred times in the business. It turned out to be a very ill-advised decision. The gas price shot up soon after. So once again timing was everything. At anything above $3 per mcf of gas, we would have made a fortune. At $2 we were not going to make any money. Losing the export route was the last straw.

So I was in the oil fracking business briefly. I was in the gas fracking business for a bit longer with EdgeMarc and Goldmans. I made no money in either case.

CHAPTER 33

# From Global to Local

PAM HAS SAID she would like me to slow down. But I never held that retirement was a great pastime. Give up too earlier and you slow down quicker. It can be a cause and effect. You can only hit so many golf balls. In my case, not very well.

I have always wanted to give back. The opportunity arose for me to do just that. Exeter Science Park was looking for a new chairman. They had been put onto me by Sir Robin Nicholson FRS, a legendary one-time non-executive director of BP. He has also been chief scientific officer to the government and member of the council of Exeter University. I said the science park in addition really needed somebody who understood data and that person was Richard Haycock. Richard had been a director of Oracle. He lived near me on the Dart River in Kingswear. I had begun speaking to him many years after leaving BAE. So the pair of us started to talk to the science park about my being chairman and Richard as a non-exec. They came back to us and said they would have us both.

It was only then that we realised that we should do some due diligence. During that process we figured out that it was a very complicated, not very happy shareholder group. It included the University of Exeter, Exeter City Council, the East Devon District Council and Devon County Council: in short, a mixture of local authorities and the University.

Funding was a problem. We felt that the executive had become too focused on building property and leasing rooms. What we were interested in was building new businesses. We did not think it was working in Exeter at the time that we were involved. So we extracted ourselves from it quite quickly, in order not to cause any damage.

Our exposure to the intellectual capital at the university spurred us to

## 33. FROM GLOBAL TO LOCAL

press forward with our idea but with a different vehicle. We asked ourselves what we could offer to the region. What could we do to help young companies? And to help young people to start interesting companies? There were three areas we were interested in. Data, of course: Richard Haycock had been responsible for creating the cloud for Oracle and his last job for them was AI. Another, because of my expertise, was low or zero carbon. We were also interested in modern health care. A lot of modern healthcare intellectual property was being created in Exeter, and at Exeter medical school. We started to talk to Roger Killen, who at the time was the Royal Society's entrepreneur in residence at Exeter University.

We thought our competitive advantage would be to raise a small fund and invest in start-up companies, providing small amounts of money, large amounts of mentoring and huge networks, none of which they had. While we were raising the fund, we were talking to small companies. We found that there were many small medical companies in Exeter. They might have needed to talk to the chief medical officer of a large pharmaceutical company. They had no clue how to go about doing it. On one occasion I was able to do so through my own network. I asked for a contact from Helge Lund. As well as being chairman of BP, he was chairman of the huge Danish healthcare company Novo Nordisk. So we were able to get this company to talk to the chief medical advisers of a massive multinational in about 24 hours. They could not have done that by themselves.

We raised a small fund QantX from high-net-worth individuals and others who were interested in the same things we were. Most of them lived on and around the Dart River. My neighbour in Devon Mark Yallop became a partner and an investor and then deputy chair of the fund; another neighbour Rod Jack was an investor. It was established as an Enterprise Investment System (EIS) and Seed Enterprise Investment Scheme (SEIS) fund. We raised about £10 million. Our intent was to invest at an early stage in intellectual property in the southwest. This was pretty small beer in comparison to the numbers I was used to dealing with but the intellectual property available in Plymouth, and particularly Exeter, Bristol, Bath and Southampton was quite extraordinary.

I had a conversation with Lincoln Bennett at Access industries. He said it was too small for them and they did not go for such early-stage funding. But Lincoln spoke to Len Blavatnik who felt he should help me out. Len was really helpful. It would have been difficult to have started without his assistance. They gave us £2 million: £1 million to create the Blavatnik innovation prize in the southwest and the other £1 million was to help us get going as working capital. We made our first modest grant to a professor who had figured out a new way to make search engines work.

Len's name gets wrongly associated with Russian oligarchs. Len's involvement in Russia was minimal. Living in London, he has American, British and Ukrainian citizenship. He is a Knight of the Realm in the United Kingdom. He put £75 million into the Blavatnik School of Government. He built the Blavatnik building for Tate Modern and has helped many other people in the art world. He had bought Warner Music. Emily was doing a great deal with the Royal Opera House. We had a wonderful evening with Len where we had dinner on the stage and the Royal Ballet danced around us. You could hear the rustling of the tutus and the shuffling of feet: it was absolutely extraordinary.

Our fund QantX began operations on 1 January 2021. One of the first tasks was to recruit advisers. We had a fantastic list of advisers. We realised quite quickly that there were a lot of really able people who had an interest in the southwest. Some might have had a house in Salcombe. Some because during lockdown or before decided to give up working in London for a better way of life in Devon and Cornwall. And some because this has always been home. Like the Earl of Devon, an IP lawyer; Dame Viv Cox, who was with me at BP; and Penny Dash, who was the healthcare partner for McKinsey. In the first couple of years we invested in nine companies. We made about five or six grants – these were from £25,000 to £50,000 – through the Blavatnik prize to up-and-coming people who we thought had near-commercial ideas. The nine companies were all doing well and we considered they would need follow-on investment. With all this happening and with a list of advisers that would pass muster with some of the largest private equity firms in the world, we realised we needed a bigger fund. So we began working on a prospectus for Fund Two.

There were two other funds elsewhere doing what we were. Northern Gritstone, a fund of around £300 million, was spearheaded by Lord O'Neill, who as Jim O'Neill had been at Goldman Sachs and then championed the Northern Powerhouse. In the Midlands, Mindforge has been under development. We wanted to become the Southwest Gritstone. A lot of venture capital from London was going to Bristol but seldom

## 33. FROM GLOBAL TO LOCAL

flowed south or west of Bristol. We also wanted to create the Greater Southwest version, so everywhere from Land's End to Southampton. The intellectual property available in the greater Southwest was really much bigger than we thought. Initially we feared we would not identify enough pipeline companies. Within a year we had a list of 150 companies. The nine first invested in were all science and engineering people from Plymouth, Exeter, Bristol, Bath and Southampton universities.

One of the companies that we first awarded a Blavatnik prize to was a company called SeaCURE. It has figured out how to remove carbon from seawater. This was one of those initiatives to help with the energy transition. At present a lot of money is being spent across the world on schemes for the direct capture of carbon from air. However the density of carbon in water is 100 times greater than the density of carbon in the air. So why wouldn't you take the seawater out of the sea, remove the carbon, put the water back in the sea, which whereupon absorbs more carbon? This was one of the companies that we were trying to mentor and bring along and help with a small grant.

Another extraordinarily interesting company we invested in was Senisca, a modern healthcare enterprise splitting mRNA to reverse the ageing of cells. It was formed by some brilliant scientists at Exeter university headed by Professor Lorna Harries. After more than 15 years at Exeter medical school researching the use of mRNA technology on cancer and the effects of ageing she formed her own company. She has won all sorts of awards. We were the first people to invest in Senisca, as individuals, even before we started the fund. There was later great interest from the cosmetic giant L'Oreal for their skin cell treatment.

The nine companies that we put money into have created over 100 new jobs. These were well-paid jobs in an area where the average income was quite low. As important as being well paid, these jobs were for the skilled or highly qualified. That meant locals did not have to leave to London or elsewhere to get the jobs to suit their high skills or expertise. That was why small companies were important.

At QantX, besides me as Chairman and Richard Haycock as CEO, we were lucky to take on Harry Alexander. He had previously been at the Royal Society, managing entrepreneurs in residence at every UK university. So his network was the right fit for us. Furthermore he trained as a chemist, a qualification that added to our existing expertise in data and engineering.

Then there were Roger Killen, who had two successful healthcare exits, and Patrick Eriksson who was an expert in early stage businesses. We were also joined by the very able Michelle Law as COO, who came to us from UBS. She was one of those people who could have worked for any private equity firm in the world. But she happened to be in Exeter for social reasons. Her job initial focus was help raising Fund 2.

I chaired the Investment Committee. I also joined the board of one of our portfolio companies, making batteries. It was set up by two former executives from British Volt who had previously worked for Dyson. They both knew a huge amount about the design of batteries. We thought that they were capable of creating IP in the battery world. We were not talking about building a giga factory. But it could still create a sizeable number of jobs. Like SeaCURE it was engaged in the energy transition.

And in early 2022 this took on even greater urgency.

CHAPTER 34

# Turning Point

THE RUSSIAN INVASION of Ukraine in February 2022 was a turning point. It changed the world we live in. And it changed the perceptions of individuals and the policies of states. With the benefit of hindsight, many are now saying that the war was inevitable, that it was foretold. They point to the Russian invasion of Crimea in 2014, and the west's minimal reaction to it. They cite Putin's talk about Ukrainians and Russians being one people. The signs might have been there. But there were those who knew Putin well who believed even very shortly before the invasion that he would not carry out his threat.

I was with Mikhail Fridman ten days before the invasion. He is a real intellectual heavyweight. He thinks widely about the world. I asked him if Putin was going to invade. Mikhail said no. I asked him why not. Because it would be economic suicide, he said. Putin would not want to be put into the hands of the Chinese.

Mikhail was against the war. He said that this war was not helpful to anybody. But then of course Mikhail is not actually Russian. He was born in Lviv, in the west of the Ukraine. But he has spent all his life dealing in and with Russia. He knew very well how things worked. I made the mistake once of asking Mikhail what the Russian government thought about a matter. He answered that I could not ask him that. I could only ask him what Putin thought. It was not helpful in my opinion to sanction Mikhail.

Why then did not he and others like him, those who had created vast fortunes for themselves in Russia, do more to influence the man who took the decisions in Russia? The answer was that it was not at all clear if anyone had any influence over Putin. What has emerged is that Putin did not listen to anyone much. He had isolated himself during the COVID pandemic. Not many had access to him. And he made clear his view of the oligarchs. As Potanin had told me, he allowed them to get on and make money so long as they did not interfere in politics.

If Putin felt that Nato was weak and divided, and Germany was too dependent on energy from Russia to take action, he severely miscalculated. The invasion helped galvanise existing Nato members and prompted other states to seek admission to the alliance. And Germany stirred itself both to cut its reliance on Russian gas and to take a more assertive position in terms of supplying Nato standard arms and military equipment to help the Ukrainians defend themselves. The decades of seeking to appease the Russians ended overnight.

The effect of the invasion also led to a re-assessment of the two industries to which I had devoted my professional life: oil and gas, and the defence sector. Before the war, the two industries were among the most vilified among certain sections of the population. The war changed that. People realised that they wanted and needed cheap and reliable energy. And it became obvious that an aggressor could not be defeated by waving white flags. An aggressor had to be met with steely defence. That required a determined leadership and committed forces. It also needed quantities of top of the range equipment and munitions. That meant higher spending on defence.

The western oil companies have been accused of complicity with oligarchs who had brazenly stolen the state assets they controlled. That we had made vast amounts of money in a naive belief that Russia would transform itself into a liberal economy. But at the time we did enter Russia, that is exactly what western government hoped and believed. We were trying to help Russia's reform programme. We were trying to bring Russia into the world economic system while making money for ourselves. It was a more open and cooperative period, before Putin achieved ascendancy – although the deal with TNK was sealed by him. The young people who embraced the change from communist organised government to a more capitalist-type market economy would not have dreamt of doing what has happened today. The invasion of Ukraine was not led by Russians in the diaspora created after 1989. It was the man from the past, who was disadvantaged in 1989 by the end of the KGB.

The Russian invasion of Ukraine, and the west's response to it, exposed

## 34. TURNING POINT

the dangerous reliance of Europe on external and above all Russian supplies of gas – for heating homes and fuelling German industry. Oil of course was easily sourced from elsewhere. But it can take years and billions of dollars to build the infrastructure to receive LNG shipments to replace the gas from the network of pipelines from Russia. Supply issues were already a challenge before the crisis. Shortly after the war broke out I had a conversation with Tony Hayward about where the world was. We agreed that the war in the Ukraine was horrible but it had accelerated existing problems in the world energy markets. It had not caused them. The supply shortages and price rises were going to happen anyway. The root cause was that investors and shareholders did not understand the energy market. Activist investors had gone overboard. Some forced the passing of resolutions at AGMs obliging the boards of banks and pension funds not to invest in oil and gas and to invest hugely in the energy transition. I believe in the energy transition. But what people did not seem to realise was that you cannot jump from 100% hydrocarbons to 100% green energy overnight. Their pressure for change helped reduce investment in energy projects. The reduction in investment in oil and gas was exacerbated by COVID. We have been investing $400 or $500 billion a year in upstream oil and gas. We all know that in order to maintain the requirement of the oil and gas industry over the next 10 or 20 or 30 years, the industry globally needs to spend much more. Even before the war in Ukraine we were seeing oil prices going up. In answer to a question I said we would see $100 a barrel oil before long.

So those people who perhaps correctly said they needed us to transition from a world of hydrocarbons to a world of no hydrocarbons must assume some accountability. The trouble was that they had absolutely no idea about the size and scale of what they were talking about and therefore the length of time to do it. As a result there has been a lack of investment so energy prices have gone up.

If you increase the pace of investment, where is the cash coming from? As far as energy companies are concerned, it has to come from things that create cash now. That is oil and gas. As a practical matter the world has to maintain energy security while investing heavily in the transition. That is the equation. The kids gluing themselves to the road do not understand that they travelled to wherever they did courtesy of a fuel. Everything in our lives is energy dependent. Oil companies provide for every aspect of life. Food. Pumping clean water and pumping out wastewater. Plastics, pharmaceuticals, fertilisers, ammonia. 70% of agriculture depends on this. As well as fuel for transport, oil and gas are used for heat and light. It has now become more difficult to manage the transition. Bernard Looney at BP had rebalanced the role of oil and gas perhaps a little too fast. The transitions for energy, and the transition for plastics, are all vitally important. They are going to need vast amounts of investment. Activists were demanding that in 2050 there must be zero oil and gas used. This was not possible. They wanted to draw a straight line from where the companies were at that time to zero. So they were asking companies like BP and Shell to basically divest each year that straight line proportion of their customers. But if the oil companies were to keep on shedding customers, then this would reduce their ability to invest in the transition. That would be mad.

We have got somehow to get the world to understand that we need a balance. I would like to see less coal and more gas as part of that transition. The world has actually reduced its consumption of gas, when it probably should have increased its consumption of gas and reduced its consumption of coal. You cannot just go from where we are today to zero hydrocarbons. It is not possible. But you can invest heavily in renewables. We can invest heavily in people who understand how to replace plastics with biological seaweed. We can make all of these investments. We probably need to do them all at a greater pace. But we will have to do it while we continue to feed people and improve the quality of life of the 7 billion people on the planet. Not to mention the 2 billion more we are going to have between now and 2050. Energy demand will soar. So far renewables have not managed to cover the increase in energy demand. That is the first thing we need to do. It is similar to the oil business, when you have to fill the hole in production from a naturally declining field first. Here we have got to fill the incremental demand with clean energy, before we start to reduce the fossil fuel elements. Part of that must be to move out of coal into gas, and out of oil into gas, as part of maintaining people's quality of life.

Just prior to the Russian invasion of Ukraine, the oil price was heading towards $100 a barrel. The gas price was increasing in Europe, though not in the United States, or not anything like as much. This led to a hugely elevated amount of dollars flying back down the pipeline to the Kremlin. The climate activists helped to fill the Kremlin's war chest. On top of this

## 34. TURNING POINT

the Ukraine situation sent prices even higher. The price of oil reached $120 a barrel although it fell back. So the people who rightly are worried about the planet actually have been part of the cause of the problem. Their action gave Putin the money to do what he has been doing. As a result too we have had low growth and high inflation. And we will have high interest rates because of high inflation.

The sanctions imposed by the west on Russia also led to BP announcing it was exiting its shareholding in Rosneft. It had acquired a 19.75% stake in 2013. This survived the Russian seizure of Crimea. BP had two directors on the board. Both resigned after the invasion of Ukraine. BP has written down the asset.

As for defence, the war in Ukraine has prompted many states in Europe to re-assess the threat posed by a militarily aggressive nationalist Russia. Many have raised their defence spending and been beefing up their armed forces after decades of assuming they would never be called upon to fight. Increasingly they came to realise they needed a stronger deterrent against an adversary that had already shown it was hostile. This required the skills and industrial base to support re-arming. It also provided employment. Missiles – infantry operated anti-tank missiles and large Storm Shadow cruise missiles – have been supplied to Ukraine made by MBDA, formed in 2001 by the main European makers of missiles systems in France, Italy and the UK, in which BAE has a 37.5% stake. BAE has also seen an increase in orders for tracked combat vehicles and other weapons systems.

The stock price rose from just over £5 at the beginning of 2022 to around £10 in 2023. This of course was more to do with the Ukraine and uncertainty in the world. I spent ten years arguing for the defence budget of the UK and other Nato members to be 3% of GDP. More is the pity we did not spend more earlier.

As I end this short account of the business aspects of a wonderful and privileged life, a decade after leaving my last big job as chairman of a FTSE company, I look forward with some concerns for the future.

The world certainly needs energy and security in large measure. It also needs peace and a low carbon world. If we have peace, cooperation and collaboration, I am confident that innovation, science and technology can fix the environmental, energy and social needs of an expanding world.

For myself, it seemed too easy an option to retire. While energy allowed, I wanted to continue with my role in banking and investment to help in my small way to address the big issues facing us all. As people age, they must keep looking to the future.

I also can look back at a wonderful career. I started my professional life building bridges or checking them for structural integrity. It was not long before I realised that my work entailed building bridges in a much broader, less concrete sense.

The role of oil and gas companies, indeed of all energy companies, is to give governments with energy resources a more competitive margin than other companies offer. It is the same principle whether we are discussing oil or gas, wind or sunshine. Energy companies must provide resource holders a good return on the development and exploitation of the resources they are blessed with. To do so, the energy companies must build huge intellectual and human bridges. Between the government and its expectations. And between the company and its expectations. That is what the negotiation is about. In a sense, every negotiation is building a bridge. And such a bridge does not get built unless the negotiation manages to span the gaps between all sides.

The most important commodity in achieving this or any other objective is empathy. Empathy is just a fancy word for connecting with people. It is getting to the place where people *want* to do what you want done, without you having to stand over them. It requires great understanding of what motivates people. People respond differently to different leadership styles. I had been running the US out of Houston for three or four months when the lovely HR guy came to me to offer me his observations about my approach. He told me most Americans did not understand my roundabout way of speaking. I needed to change my language to be more American. I am not sure I ever actually did that. But it was a lesson in the crucial importance of understanding others, whether your own employees of your customers, all those you interact with, especially from different cultures, in order to communicate effectively to achieve the results you desired.

You have to have the appropriate empathy for the person you are talking to or people you are trying to engage. The proof that it worked was the magic we created during the five or six years I was running BP exploration. This derived from building the bridges between myself and the executive management and between the Executive Committee and the 18,000 people making decisions in every continent of the world, every day and every night. We had such understanding that it reached the point where people knew what I wanted before I even had to articulate what it was that I wanted. One example stands out in my mind. We had an issue with how to drill in Angola. It was just after we had won an award for extended drilling at Endicott: it was the longest reach drilling in the world to date. I wanted to ask the guys in Alaska to jump on a plane and show the Angola team how it could be done. When I raised the idea, I was told that the Alaskan team had already done just that. I was so impressed. It showed how teams were working horizontally, learning off each other and mentoring each other. That illustrates how we achieved this extraordinary result. On every important metric we were better than any oil company in the world. We had the highest cash flow per barrel. We had the lowest lifting cost per barrel. We were putting more reserves on the balance sheet than any other company. At one time we were booking twice the number of reserves that we produced. If you can do that you can grow. The results were measured by physics and mathematics. But they were made possible by people, and why and how they performed so exceptionally. And that came down to empathy and building those bridges.

This is a roundabout way of saying that the most important bridges I ever built were between people.

At BAE, I was not the person who was emotionally leading the 100,000 people employed by the company. But I took responsibility for building bridges between the board and the executive; between the company and shareholders; and between the company and governments, particularly in the UK and US. In the final chapter of my working life, in the post-corporate phase as it were, I was able to establish links and create opportunities for others.

So in many ways my life came full circle. My early career owed much to the mentoring and guidance of those I worked for. It has been only fitting that in my turn, across the span of my own life, I have been able to do the same to newer generations. Building bridges between old and new. And, I hope, making some magic.

# ENDNOTES

1. As amply set out in 2004 BAE Annual report
2. '[Olver] also commented that non-executive involvement was woeful when he discussed strategy. They did not have a clue what the strategy was.' [Oliver Morgan. Industrial Editor. *The Observer*. 14 November 2004]
3. "Mr. Straw: The Secretary of State [Condoleeeza Rice] received a presentation from Mr. Mike Turner, the chief executive officer of BAE Systems. Those who know him will know that he is no wilting violet, and he was able to put his position politely but firmly." [https://publications.parliament.uk/pa/cm200506/cmhansrd/vo060425/debtext/60425-02.htm] 25 Apr 2006
4. This was acknowledged in an interview Mike and I gave jointly to the FT. "The row became so bad that when Sir Richard Evans, the long-serving BAE chairman and a mentor to Mr Turner, announced he was leaving, there emerged what one person close to the situation calls 'a huge whispering campaign in the Whitehall system: there's a new chairman coming in, Turner must go'. Mr Olver acknowledges he got an earful when he made his initial rounds at the MoD." *BAE's contrasting top brass see eye to eye* 6 September 2005
5. "The Nominations Committee and the Board have reviewed the provisions in the revised Code and have concluded that since the beginning of 2004, under the definitions used, six of the current non-executive directors are independent and one, Lord Hesketh, is not ... because he ... has been on the Board for more than ten years with effect from the beginning of 2004. As a result, at least half of the Board does not comprise independent non-executive directors as proposed in the revised Code. The Nominations Committee and the Board are aware of this and will be taking it into consideration in their plans for the future composition of the Board." [2003 Annual Report, 25 Feb 2004]
6. 24 April 2005
7. Aviation Weekly 11 July 2005
8. *The Independent*. Michael Harrison, Business Editor. Tuesday 28 March 2006
9. *An Uncommon Lawyer*. Rt Hon Lord Woolf, CH. p120
10. *Idem*. p 119

11. *BAE's contrasting top brass see eye to eye* FT 6 September 2005
12. *Idem*
13. 'Sir Richard Evans retired as a director and Chairman on 30 June 2004. He remained employed in a part-time customer relationship role and ceased to be an employee on 29 February 2008. In 2008, his remuneration was £265,480 (2007 £332,400) and comprised a salary, a cash allowance for a car, chauffeur-driven car and consultancy fees for his role as a member of the Home Market Advisory Board for Saudi Arabia'. [2008 BAE Annual Report p92]
14. Michael Harrison profile in *Brunswick Review*, Issue 8 Spring 2014.
15. 'The BAE executives believe they face a dilemma in co-operating with the US probe. If they do so, they risk being in breach of the UK Official Secrets Act. Co-operation would therefore require UK government permission – and there is no evidence that this has so far been forthcoming. "The government couldn't release them from the provisions" of the act, Mr Howarth said.' FT 14 July 2008 *Tory Protests over handling of BAE trio* Stephen Fidler, Defence and Security Editor.
16. Board members visited Oman and Saudi Arabia in 2008. 2008 Annual Report p 73
17. A detailed version of these constantly changing configurations from the point of view of the MoD was supplied by the former head of defence procurement, Sir Bernard Gray: 'Whitehall mandarins did not cripple Britain's aircraft carriers' 1 August 2022 *Daily Telegraph*
18. 'The original al-Yamamah contract is a government-to-government document and the DoJ is believed to have found it difficult to gather facts as the details are classified as secret by the UK government, according to legal sources.' *BAE's Turner lands up at Babcock*. FT 27 May 2008
19. 'BAE knows that negotiations there can take more than a decade and that New Delhi has a habit of changing its mind'. FT 12 November 2013
20. '"BAE" documents lost by SFO found at cannabis farm.' *The Daily Telegraph*. 13 September 2013
21. "I am not sure that we would say that we have lost business. We would not undertake business that we thought we could not do in an appropriate fashion. We have made informed decisions as to what our risk appetite will allow us to do and where we consider that the market, the opportunity or the nature of the transaction is not one that we are willing to work with or engage in." Joanna Talbot, BAE Chief Counsel Compliance and Regulation, to the House of Lords Select Committee on the Bribery Act 2010. Oral evidence Tuesday 3 July 2018

ACKNOWLEDGEMENTS

WHILST THE WORDS in *Building Bridges* are my own, I couldn't have done it without the input from many others.

So, I would like to thank Philip Bramwell, Roddy Kennedy, Peter Bevan, and Jack Golden, who have all read some or all of the book, for their comments and corrections to the text; Charles Richards for help with editing; Cressida Hogg for her support; my brother Tim for his photos and research into the family history; my daughters Claire and Kate for their encouragement and comments; and Janet Ling for her customary efficiency and support.

BP Archives gave unstinting help in finding photographs and then kindly granted permission to use them. I also thank *The Times/* News Licensing for permission to reproduce cartoons from *The Times* and *The Sunday Times*.

I showed my manuscript to a number of former colleagues and people with whom I've worked, and they were kind enough to be complimentary. My thanks to Sir Sherard Cowper-Coles, Bernard Looney, Sir John Manzoni and the Rt Hon Lord Woolf for allowing me to repeat their generous endorsements on the cover and elsewhere.

I am especially grateful to Lord Gold for graciously agreeing to write the Foreword.

Rupert Cowper-Coles has constantly provided sound advice and been a firm hand on the legal tiller during the whole project.

I also wish to thank Ed Gelsthorpe, general counsel at BAE, for his critical comments on a draft of the book. His detailed critique spurred me to go back and clarify some key points, to provide more telling evidence to support my assertions and to underscore what a mess I had found BAE in and what I and my team did to clear it up. Much of what I did was already in the public domain, as the endnotes attest. I added my own perspective of why we did what we did.

Once books have been written they need to be typeset and designed and they also need a striking cover – for these elements of the publishing process my thanks go to Lyn Davies. Finally, I pay tribute to the calm and professional hand of my publisher, Anthony Weldon, who guided us home through some at times choppy waters.

# INDEX

Abdullah bin Abdulaziz, King of Saudi Arabia 119, 150
Abu Dhabi 10, 15, 63-5, 73, 139
Access Industries 157
Addenbrooke's 28
Aiken, Phil 42
Air Alaska 20
Airbus 115, 133, 142, 144-5
Aircraft carriers 83, 96, 114-5
Al-Mubarak, Khaldoon Khalifa 64
Al-Yamamah 115, 117, 119, 132
Alaska 10, 12-21, 26, 36-41, 44-46, 53-6, 60, 70, 73, 79, 167
Alberta 11
Alderman, Richard 133
Alexander, Harry 159
Alexander, Ralph 42
Alexandria 4
Alfa Bank 110
Algeria 65-6, 78-9
Allen, Dr David 21-2, 77
Allseas 49
Alyeska 20-1
Amberjack deepwater field 41
Amoco 54-6, 59, 61-2, 68, 74-5
Anchorage 19-20, 58
Anderson, Paul 140

Andrew Field 48-9, 114
Andrew, Prince, Duke of York 148
Anglo-Iranian Oil Company 15
Anti-Bribery Convention 91
APA Holdings 153
Apache 153
Apprenticeship Taskforce 80
Arab oil boycott 18
Arab oil embargo 46
Arab oil producers 10
ARCO *see* Atlantic Richfield
Arctic 16-17, 23, 38
Arizona 21, 33
Ashburton, Lord 37
Astute-class submarine 87
Athabasca oil sands 11
Athenaeum 117
Atlantic Richfield (ARCO) 16-17, 20-1, 26, 45, 56, 59, 62-3, 68
Atlantis 61
Auckland 25
Australia 79, 124
Avignon 45
Azerbaijan 71, 73, 79

BA 55
Babcock 114

## INDEX

Bach, Lord 85
BAE 62, 80-101, 113-153, 156, 165, 167
BAE Systems *see* BAE
Bahamas 106
Baku 71
Balfour Beatty 153
Balzer, Dick 33, 58, 60, 75
Bangalore 139
Bank of England 66
Barber, Lionel 124
Baring family 37
Barrow-in-Furness 87, 98
BART (Bay Area Rapid Transit) 22
Bath 157, 159
Beaufort Sea 16, 26
Beechcraft King Air 13
BEIS 137
Bell, Tim 94
Bell Pottinger 94
Bennett, Lincoln 157
Bering sea 16
Berlin 144
Berlin wall 105
Bethlehem, Sir Daniel 119
BHP 42-3, 61
Black Rock 3
Blair, Tony 53, 83, 95, 108, 111, 116, 135, 138
Blavatnik, Len 110, 143, 157-9, 
Blyth, Chay 68-9, 102
Boeing 142, 144, 146
Bogdanov, Vladimir 109
Bottrell, Tony 102
Bowen, Desmond 84
Bowlin, Mike 45, 56
Box girder bridge 8-10
BP 1-2, 9, 10-27, 30-79, 80, 81, 82, 84, 86, 88, 90, 92, 94, 98, 105-112, 114, 129, 140, 147, 151, 152, 153, 154, 156, 157-8, 164, 165, 166
*BP Explorer* 67-9, 102
BP Nutrition 35
BP Shipping 54
Bramwell, Philip 100-1, 119
Brentford 4
Bristol 157, 158, 159
Britannic House 10, 35, 70
British Aerospace 97
British Antarctic Survey 23
British Gas 31
British Petroleum *see* BP
British Virgin Islands 22
British Volt 160
Britoil 30-1
Brooks Range 16
Browder, Bill 106
Brown and Root 49
Brown, Gordon 80, 127, 135, 138, 140
Browne, John 26, 31-4, 39, 40, 42, 48, 54, 56, 74, 76-8, 80-2, 94, 105, 106, 109, 148
Bruce Field 31
Buchanan, John 25, 76, 77, 152
Buckee, Jim 23
Buckingham Palace 119, 148
Budapest 6
Budd, Julia 99
Budock Vean 3
Burma railway 8
Burnham-on-Crouch 7
Bush, George W 95, 96, 127
Business Council for Britain 135
Butler, Nick 84

C-Span 56
Ca's Xorc 117

Cable and Wireless 36
Cadets 6
Cairns, Earl 134
Cairo Conference (1921) 128
Calgary 11-12, 47
California 21-2, 26, 56
Cambridge 1, 23, 28
Cameron, David 132, 135, 137, 139, 143, 151
Canada 11-12, 23, 38, 47, 153
Cape Verde 103
Caribbean 22
Caribou 18, 53
Carlton Gardens 86
Carlyle 153
Carroll, Phil 99, 129, 139
Cartellieri, Ulrich 94
Cazenove 100
CD&R *see* Clayton, Dubilier & Rice
CDC 134
Ceyhan 71
Chase, Rodney 36, 48, 82
Chelsea 54
Cheney, Dick 64-5, 95
Chernogorneft 107, 108
Chicago 54, 55
Chigwell 5
Chirag 71
Chubais, Anatoly 105-6
*Churchill's Folly* 128
City University 7
Clarke, Ken 132
Clayton, Dubilier & Rice 98, 153-4
Cleddau bridge 9
Cleveland 38, 39
Clinton, Bill 46, 139
Coca-Cola 118
Colombia 44, 63, 70, 74, 78

Combined Code on governance 89, 96
Communications Council of America 45
Confederation of British Industry 108
Congress 20, 32, 44-5, 47
Conoco 41, 56
ConocoPhillips *see* Conoco
Control Risks 70
Cook, Lod 21
Cornwall 3-6, 158
Corporate Planning, BP 25-6, 34
Cowper-Coles, Sir Sherard 115, 140
Cox, Dame Viv 158
Crane, Sheena 97
Crimea 105, 161, 165
Crossrail 153
Cusiana 44, 71
Cyprus 63
Czech Republic 119

Daft, Doug 118
*Daily Telegraph* 4
Daly, Mike 64
Darden School 24
Dart river 156, 157
Dash, Penny 158
David Mayhew 100
Deadhorse 19, 45
Denton, Mark 69
Department of Justice (US) 119, 125-6, 131-3, 148
Detica 130
Devon 157-8
Devon County Council 156
Devon, Earl of 158
Diageo 140, 153
Dingell, Congressman John 44-5
Dingman, Michael 106
DoJ *see* Department of Justice (US)

# INDEX

Dorchester, the 130
Dowdy, John 83
Drinkwater, Anne 153
Du Plessis, Jan 122
Dudley, Bob 54, 74, 111
Dulwich 4, 5
Dyson, Sir James 136, 160

EADS 143, 145-6
Eagle Ford 154
Easington 10
East Bay 22
East Devon District Council 156
EdgeMarc 154-5
Edgewater 154
Egon Zehnder 97, 122
Egypt 56, 59
El Alamein 4
Elf 110
Emotional Intelligence (EQ) 24, 58, 69,
Emtunga 49
Enders, Tom 143-4
England 11-12, 117, 135
Enhanced Oil Recovery (EOR) 23
Enron 52-3
Equinor 153
Erasmus programme 53
Essex 5-6, 19
Essex County Council 8-9
Eurofighter 87
Evans, Sir Dick 80, 82-4, 87, 89, 121
Exco *see* Executive Committee
Executive Committee 33-4, 59-60, 62, 73-4, 166
Exeter 156, 157, 159, 160
Exeter Science Park 156
Exeter University 156

Exim bank 108
Exxon 16-17, 20-21, 38-9, 45-6, 61-2, 71, 153
Eyers, Simon 153

F-35B 130
F-35C 130
Fairbanks 19
Falcon 7X 144
Falcon 50 38
Falmouth 3
*Falmouth Packet* 3
Farnsworth, Jim 41
FBI 126
Federal Trade Commission 54, 56-7
*Financial Times* 124, 125
FitzGerald, Niall 129
Fluor 99
Ford 106
Ford's Theater 95
Foreign Corrupt Practices Act (US) 91, 110
Fortune 500 22
Fossum, Martin 154
Foster Back, Philippa 118
Fridman, Mikhail 107, 109, 110, 112, 161
FTC *see* Federal Trade Commission
Fyfield 5

GEC Marconi 97, 100
Geological Society 11
Germany 145, 152, 153, 162
Gibson-Smith, Chris 26, 152
Gilvary, Brian 153
Glasgow 12, 30, 31, 47
*Glasgow* 103
Gleacher Shacklock 142
Glencore 152

175

Global Challenge 67-8
Glocer, Tom 52
Glover, General Sir Jimmy 37
Gold, David 132
Golden, Jack 39, 74, 107, 154
Goldman Sachs 77, 83, 87, 98, 154-5, 158
Good Friday Agreement (1998) 63
Gore, John 46, 56
Gould, Andrew 122, 152
Gove, Michael 136-7
GP14 6
Gran Canarias 102
Grand Military Gold Cup 119
Greece 144
Green party 145
Green, Harriet 140
Green, Stephen 151
Greenbank Terrace 3, 6
GSK 104
Gulf of Mexico 26, 38-43, 44, 47, 61, 65, 70, 73, 79, 147
Gulf War (1991) 36, 78, 95
Gulliver, Stuart 151
Gunashli 71
GUPCO 59

Hagle, George 20
Hammond, Philip 143
Hampton, Philip 104
Hancock, Matt 137
Hannay, David 63
Hanoi 67
Harbour Energy 153
Harding, James 124
Harries, Professor Lorna 159
Hartnall, Michael 80, 88, 129
Harvard 25, 110

Haycock, Richard 156, 157, 159
Hays 97
Hayward, Tony 77, 152, 163
Heathrow 13
Helford river 3
Helios 68
Henley Management School 69
Herbert Smith lawyers 132
Hermit of Siberia 109
Hermitage Fund 106
Hesketh, Lord 89, 97
Hewitt, Patricia 84
Heywood, Jeremy 83, 135, 147
Highlands Fabricators 49
Hill Street 30, 36
Hill, the 20, 47
HMG 31, 150
Ho Ching 92-3
Hogg, Cressida 82
Hogg, Sir Christopher 51, 82, 129
Holt, Tim 154
Hong Kong 4
Hoon, Geoffrey 84
Hopwood, Andy 153
Horton, Bob 26, 30, 31, 37, 40, 82
Horton, Sally 36
House Energy and Commerce Committee 44
House of Representatives 20, 44
Houston 38, 47, 77, 126, 166
HSBC 4, 132, 151-3
Hudson, Linda 140
Humber 10
Hungarian uprising 6

Iceman, The 23
Imperial War Museum 4
Imrie, Alastair 83, 84, 100

# INDEX

In Amenas 66
India 129, 139
Individual Development Plan (IDP) 15
Indonesia 55, 63, 79
Ineos Energy 153
Ingenious Films 147
Inglis, Andy 74, 77, 129, 139
Invesco 145
Iran 10, 11, 15, 16, 71, 127-8
Iran Libya Sanctions Act 71
Iran Oil Services Company 11
Iran Sanctions Act 71
Iraq 10, 15, 32, 64-5, 78, 95, 128
Irian Jaya 63
Irkutsk 106
Isles of Scilly 69
Italy 26, 165

Jack, Rod 157
Jaguars 92
Janet *see* Ling
Japanese 8, 18
Jarvis, Dr Richard 118
Jenner, Hannah 102
Joint Strike Fighter (JSF) 95-6, 130-1

Kazakhstan 122
KBR 114
Kennedy, Roddy 94
Kennicott 36
Kent, Professor Sir Peter 11
KGB 162
Khan, German 110
Khodorkovsky, Mikhail 109
Kidd, David 122
Kier 7
King, Ian 122-3
King's 4

Kingswear 156
Knighthood 81, 147-8
Knowles, Tony 46
Kovytka 106
Kuparuk Field 26
Kuwait 10, 15, 17, 32, 78,

La Rochelle 68
Lagardère family 143
Lake family 3-4
Lake, Ivan 3
Lancaster House 111
Lance, Ryan 56
Las Palmas 102
Law, Michelle 160
Lay, Ken 52
Lazenby, Terry 11
Lester, Michael 100-1
Lewis, Joe 106, 108
Libya 10, 71
Ling, Janet 81, 86-7, 117, 137, 153
Lithuania 112
Lockheed Martin 144
Long Island Sound 22
Longwell, Harry 45, 71
Lower 48 15, 26, 38, 55
Lucas, Dale 14, 21
Lund, Helge 157
Lviv 161
Lyford Cay 106

MI8 8
Macondo 42, 68
Mad Dog 41-2, 61, 77
Maguire, Bob 54, 153
Mallorca 117
Mandela, Nelson 59, 138
Manning, Sir David 84

177

Manson, Alastair 21-2
Manzoni, John 77-8, 153
Marathon Oil 31
Marconi 97
Margaux 128
Marks and Spencer 151
Mars Project 39-40
Mason, Sir Peter 80, 83, 88, 94, 129
Mayfair 30
MBDA 165
McDonnell Douglas 144
MCI Worldcom 75
McIntire, Lee 140
McKay, Lamar 54, 153
McKenzie, Andrew 152
McKinsey 58, 83, 87, 158
Mecca, Sharif of 128
Meggs, Tony 153
Merchant Marine Act (the Jones Act), 1920 46
Merkel, Angela 144-5, 151
Metherell, Julian 77, 154
Meynell, Luke 151
MFG *see* Motor Fuel Group
Middle East war (October 1973) 10
Middlesex 4
Milford Haven 9
Miliband, Ed 138
Milne Point 41
Mindforge 158
Minge, John 67
Ministry of Defence (MoD) 84-5, 114
Mitchell, George 63
Mittal, Lakshmi 143
Mobil 54, 62
Mogford, Steve 86
Mongstad refinery 10
Moorgate 10

*More Magic* 86, 102
Moreno, Glen 151
Morgan Stanley 54, 83, 87
Moscow 94, 105, 107, 109, 111, 127
Moses, Sir Alan (Lord Justice Moses) 116
Mossadek 15
Motor Fuel Group (MFG) 153
Mount Denali 19
Mount McKinley 19
MRH 153
Mubadala 64
Muhammad bin Zayed, Shaikh 64-5, 139
Mukluk 26
Murkowski, Frank 56
Nato 112, 144, 162, 165
Nemtsov, Boris 105, 107
Neptune 43
*New Civil Engineer* magazine 1
New York 21-2, 47, 52, 109, 126, 154
New Zealand 68
NGO 63, 65, 101
Nicholson, Sir Robin, FRS 156
Nightingale secondary school 5
Nimrod 135
Ninian pipeline 13
Nixon, Richard 18
Nobre 36
Nolan, Pete 154
Norris, Geoffrey 84
North Africa 5, 10, 63, 154
North Sea 10, 30-1, 40, 48, 50, 67
North Slope 16, 19
Northampton College of Advanced Technology 7
Northern Gritstone 158
Norway 10

Novak, Dave 153
Novo Nordisk 157
Nyquist, Scott 58, 60, 83
O'Donnell, Gus 116, 118-19, 135
O'Hare 55
O'Neill, Jim 158
O2 100
Odessa 110
OECD 91, 124
Old Greenwich 22
Olver, Captain Graham Lake 4
Olver, Claire 2, 11, 22, 28-9, 102
Olver, Jacob 3
Olver, Kate 11-12, 29
Olver, Michael 4
Olver, Pam (née Larkin) 1-2, 7, 11-12, 22, 28, 38, 44, 54, 68, 94, 117, 156
Olver, Tim 5
Oman 92, 127-8
Oracle 156-7
Oxford 1, 21, 25, 137

Pakistan 73-4
Paniguian, Richard 54
Papua New Guinea 58, 63
Parker, Sir John 138, 143
Pearson 151
Pennyhill Park 87
Pentagon 143-4
Persian Gulf 71
Phoenix 21, 33, 59
Phoenix Hotel 33
Placid 39
Plymouth 157, 159
Portillo, Michael 98
Portsmouth 101
Portugal 152
Potanin, Vladimir 106-7, 162

Powell, Jonathan 84, 135
President's Medal 138
Princeton 39
Project 1990 32, 49
Project Winter 26
Prudhoe Bay 10, 16-21, 26, 39, 46, 56
Purina Mills 36
Putin, Vladimir 67, 94, 105, 107-8, 111, 161-2, 165
QantX 157-9
Qatar 15, 52, 127
Quarta, Roberto 98, 129, 139, 153
Quarterly Performance Review (QPR) 33, 62, 67
*Queen Mary II* 126
Queen, the 111, 119

Radio Four 70
Raytheon 144
Red Crown Lodge 55, 112
Regulator 20, 56, 61
Reuter, Paul 51
Reuters 51-3, 82, 111, 118, 129
Reynolds, Paula Rosput 140
Rio Tinto (RTZ) 122, 151
Robertson, George 112, 116
Robertson, Simon 83
Robey, Simon 83
Robinson, Ralph 28-9
Rocky Mountains 11
Roding river 5
Rolls-Royce 80, 83, 116, 133
Rommel 4
Rose, Nick 140
Rose, Stuart 151
Roseland 3
Rosneft 165
Rosput *see* Reynolds

Ross, James 14
Rosslyn 102
Rotterdam 13
Royal Academy of Engineering 8, 135-8
Royal Corinthian Yacht Club 7
Royal Navy 83, 87, 114
Royal Ocean Racing Club 69
Royal Ordnance Corps 4
RTZ *see* Rio Tinto Zinc
Rudd, Sir Nigel 126, 129
Russell Reynolds *see* Reynolds
Russia 54, 71, 82, 105-112, 145, 154, 158, 161-5

Saddam Hussein 32, 64-5
Saint, John 12
St Austell 3
St Anthony 3
St James's 153
St James's Square 86
St Lucia 102
St Petersburg 108
St Stephen 3
St Vincent Street 30
Saipem 49
Salcombe 158
Salman, Prince (later King), bin Abdulaziz Al Saud 140-1
San Francisco 14, 20, 22, 47
Sand Hill Petroleum 154
Sandown Park 120
Sandwich course 8
Sardinia 36
SAS 44, 66
Savoy 109
Scatsta airport 13
Schlumberger 122
Schröder, Gerhard 110

Scotland 10, 30, 35
SeaCURE 159-60
Sears, Bill 38-9
Second Front 4
Senate, the U.S. 20, 45, 56
Senate Energy Committee 45, 56
Senisca 159
Serious Fraud Office 81, 90, 101, 113, 115-6, 119, 131-3, 148-9
Seville 77
SFO *see* Serious Fraud Office
Shacklock, Tim 142
Shaikh Zayed Al Nahyan of Abu Dhabi 64
Shelbourne, Sir Philip 30
Shell 39, 40, 50, 61, 75, 99, 153, 164
Shetlands 13
Sibneft 106
Sicily 4
Sidanco 106-8, 110, 112
Simon, David 32, 37, 48, 53
Singapore 92
Singh, Manmohan 139
Skilling, Jeffrey 52
Sloan programme 26
Smith, Paul 153
Sohio *see* Standard Oil of Ohio
Sommerfield, Ashley 97
South America 55
South Korea 54
Southampton 68, 69, 94, 157, 159
Soviet Union 6, 71, 72, 105-6
Spaghetti Junction 8
Spain 141, 152
Standard Oil of New Jersey 16
Standard Oil of Ohio (Sohio) 17, 20-1, 26-7, 38-9
Stanford 24, 26

State Department, US 133
Steel, Sir David 22
Stirling Square 86, 149
Stirrup, Jock 92, 96
Straw, Jack 85
Suez 59, 92
Suez crisis 15
Sullom Voe Terminal 13
*Sunday Times* 94, 98
Surgut 109
Surgutneftegaz 109
Surrey 88
Sutherland, Peter 53, 55, 77, 82, 98
Sydney 67, 68
Symon, Carl 129

Tacoma Narrows 9
Talisman 153
Tangguh 63, 79, 90
Tangguh Independent Advisory Panel (TIAP) 63, 90
Tanzania 119, 133-4
TAPS *see* Trans Alaska Pipeline
Tate Modern 158
Tebbit, Sir Kevin 84
Temasek 92
Thales 114
Thatcher, Margaret 30, 32, 94
Thunder Horse 41, 42, 61
*Times, The* 124
TNK-BP 82, 105-112, 127, 154, 162
Tobruk 4
Total 110
Trafalgar House 49
Trans Alaska Pipeline 17, 20-1, 56
Transjordan 128
Trinidad 56, 62-3, 79

Trinidad Petroleum Development (TPD) 12
Trinity House 3
Truss, Liz 136-7
Truro 3
Tullow 153
Turkey 71
Turner, Mike 80, 83-6, 94, 104, 121, 126
Typhoon 87, 139, 142, 150
Tyumen Oil Company *see* TNK-BP
Tyumenskaya Neftyanaya Kompaniya *see* TNK-BP

UBS 160
UK Bribery Act 124
UK continental shelf 79
Union Texas 59
United Defense 99
Unstead, Mike 23
Uppal, Ravi 129, 139
Urban, Scott 75, 154

Vadera, Shriti 127, 138
Valdez 17-19
Vann, Ian 50, 74
Vastar 59
Vekselberg, Victor 110
Vetco 103
Vietnam 52, 67-8
Virgin Islands, British 22
Virgin Islands, US 46
Virginia, University of 24
Volga river 112
VSO 134

W & C French 7-8
Wager, Chris 41

*181*

Walker, Sir David 52, 118, 125
Walnut Creek 22
Walters, Sir Peter 26, 31
Wanstead 5
Wapping 122
Warburg Pincus 153
Warshaw Robey 83
Washington DC 20, 45-6, 84, 95, 108, 126, 127, 133
Watergate building 45
Weinberg, Peter 98
Weinstock, Lord 100
West Hatch Technical High School 5
Western Approaches 69
Western Desert 4
Wharton 87, 123
Whitehall 108
Wintershall Dea 153
Wisconsin 55, 112
Wolf Rock 69
Woodford Green 5
Woodford, Neil 145
Wooley, Bill 86
Woolf report 123-5
Woolf, Lord (Harry) 117, 118-9, 124-5

Yachtmaster 86
Yahoo 127
Yallop, Mark 157
Yilmaz, Barbara 41-2

Zawawi, Dr Omar 128
Zygos 99